SPECIAL PAPERS IN INTERNATIONAL ECONOMICS

No. 9, DECEMBER 1970

POLICIES FOR INTERNAL

AND

EXTERNAL BALANCE

MARINA VON NEUMANN WHITMAN

INTERNATIONAL FINANCE SECTION

DEPARTMENT OF ECONOMICS

PRINCETON UNIVERSITY · 1970

Printed in the United States of America

PREFACE

This monograph is intended as an analytical survey of the literature on the problem of internal-external balance, a body of analysis which has been developed over the course of the past two decades. Any author of a survey faces a peculiar occupational hazard; that, in trying to include the latest contributions to his particular field of interest, he may become enmeshed in a process which resembles a dog chasing his own tail, and is just as futile. In order to avoid such a fate, I have set a firm cut-off date, taking no responsibility for the inclusion of anything published after the end of 1969. Those works in the list of references which bear a 1970 publication date are there only because I was fortunate enough to see them in a pre-publication version.

In writing this monograph, I have incurred a large number of intellectual debts, not the least of which are to the authors whose contributions I have here attempted to describe. These names appear, of course, in the list of references at the end of this study. But some of them appear also on a second list, of those whose comments and criticisms on earlier versions of this monograph shed light on many dark spots and led the author out of a number of blind alleys. Among those who were particularly helpful in this connection are Jay Levin, John Morton, Jack Ochs, Don Roper, David Starrett and, above all, Peter Kenen and Norman Miller, who have once again proved themselves friends and critics extraordinary. All of the aforementioned must, of course, be absolved of any association with the dark spots and blind alleys which remain.

M. v.N. W.

Washington, D.C.
September 1970

iii

CONTENTS

v

Policies for Internal and
External Balance

I. GENERAL CONCEPTS

A. *Internal and External Balance: From Automatic Adjustment to Policy Goals*

With the publication of his *General Theory* more than thirty years ago, John Maynard Keynes dealt a fatal blow to the classical notion that "internal balance," or full-employment equilibrium in the domestic economy, could be reached and maintained through the free play of market forces, with government intervention limited to the maintenance of a reasonable approximation to the conditions of perfect competition. But the notion that automatic adjustment mechanisms operate to assure "external balance," or equilibrium in the balance of payments, has persisted; even today, textbook treatment of the subject is devoted primarily to discussion of the "automatic" price and income effects which tend to restore balance-of-payments equilibrium after a disturbance.

This view is also shifting drastically, however, under the combined pressure of modern economic theory and observation of the chronic international financial difficulties that plague the real world under fixed exchange rates. We have come to recognize that the automatic "classical" price-adjustment process may be inoperative in a Keynesian world of unemployment and downward rigidity of wages and prices. Moreover, we know that there are real economic costs involved in automatic adjustment via income changes.[1] Therefore, central banks

---

[1] The standard Keynesian foreign-trade-multiplier analysis implies that the automatic balance-of-payments adjustment process will be incomplete for a "stable" economy, that is, one which has a positive marginal propensity to save. Mundell [24], however, argues that the adjustment process will be complete even in such cases because of the effect of induced changes in the money supply on expenditures and imports. The effects of monetary changes on real variables are not incorporated into standard multiplier theory.

today neutralize the impact of reserve changes on the money supply and thus prevent the movement of reserves resulting from a payments imbalance from having an equilibrating effect on either income or prices. Acknowledging these facts, economists have come to regard "external balance"—that is, balance-of-payments equilibrium—as one of the specific economic objectives of deliberate governmental action, rather than as something that will take care of itself.

Two of the major innovators in developing a formal body of analysis incorporating these views are Meade [21] and Tinbergen [39]. In books with almost identical titles on the theory of economic policy and both published in the early 1950's, they independently developed similar approaches to the problem of simultaneously achieving external and internal (full employment and price stability) balance via *quantitative* economic policy, that is, changing the values of existing policy parameters.[2] Their approach is to *invert* the traditional method of problem solving.[3] In the traditional "positive" or "forecasting" model, policy instruments are among the "exogenous changes" whose magnitudes are given, whereas the economic targets are the unknowns for which the system must be solved. This is the approach of multiplier analysis and, more broadly, of analysis concerned with the effects on income, employment, and the balance of payments of changes in any exogenously determined parameter, including changes which take the form of some politically desirable government action, such as a change in the tax rate or the interest rate. The Meade-Tinbergen policy model "inverts" this approach by taking some desired level of real income (that is, employment) and the balance of payments as given and then solving the system for the corresponding values of the policy variables (for example, the appropriate tax rate).

B. The Linear Targets-Instruments Model: Requirements for Solution

The targets-instruments framework developed by Meade and Tinbergen requires that we set out a system of equations that represents

---

[2] Tinbergen notes [39, p. 2] that this model ". . . is not suited to the analysis of qualitative policy . . . involving the changing of certain *qualitative* aspects of economic structure."

[3] Meade's book actually incorporates both the traditional and the inverted approach. It begins with a conventional analysis of the income and price effects of various exogenous disturbances to the balance of payments in a Keynesian-type economy where the government pursues a "neutral" or passive economic policy. It moves quickly, however, to a detailed consideration of these same processes of adjustment when governments actively pursue policies to maintain or restore both internal and external balance, pointing out that the achievement of both goals may be impossible under a system of fixed exchange rates.

the structural relationships between target variables and policy variables in a particular economy. Because their analysis rests on the simplifying assumption that the influences of both policy and exogenous variables on the target variables are linear in the neighborhood of the relevant values, the reduced form of a system of this type can be represented in matrix form as $y = Aw + Bx$. The y's represent the target variables, the x's the policy-instrument variables, and the w's the exogenous or disturbance variables which are outside the direct control of the government authorities. The matrix A consists of a_{ij} coefficients representing the quantitative effects of the various disturbances on the target variables, and the B matrix is composed of b_{ij} coefficients representing the effects of the policy variables, for a particular economy. Except under special conditions,[4] such a system will be interdependent; each instrument will affect all the targets simultaneously.

Perhaps the most obvious requirement for the achievement of the desired values of target variables in a system such as we are describing is that the policy instruments utilized be effective in their impact on the target variables. An attempt to achieve internal and external balance is doomed to failure if one of the instruments employed is a tariff on peanut butter, however high it may be set.

Some difficulties arise, however, when we try to express precisely what is meant by the "effectiveness" of a particular policy instrument with respect to a particular target variable. Generally speaking, a policy instrument is more effective the larger the change in the target variable achieved by a given change in the policy variable, or the smaller the change in the policy variable required to bring about a given change in the target variable. This sounds very much as if we are simply stating the same criterion two different ways. But an examination of the underlying logical structure reveals that they may not come to the same thing at all.

If one takes what Tinbergen calls the "traditional" approach, regarding the targets as unknown functions of the given policy parameters, the effectiveness of instrument x_j with respect to target y_i is $\delta y_i / \delta x_j$, which appears to correspond to the first definition given

[4] The special conditions prevail when the coefficient matrices are either diagonal or triangular or block-diagonal or block-triangular, implying that the system can either be partitioned into self-contained subsystems or arranged into systems of one-way causal relationships. For a discussion of such systems and their implications for the decentralization of policy-making, see Fox, Sengupta, and Thorbecke [8, pp. 24-25].

above. If the problem is inverted, the values of the instrument variables become the unknowns, dependent upon the predetermined desired values of the target variables. Now the logical measure of the same effectiveness is $\frac{1}{\delta x_j/\delta y_i}$, analogous to the second part of the verbal definition.[5] These two expressions will be the same only under very special circumstances; in the general case, when all targets and all variables are interdependent, they are sure to differ.

Tinbergen [39] offers an example to illustrate this point, using a simple macroeconomic model and data for the Netherlands in 1949. Using the first concept of effectiveness, $\delta y_i/\delta x_j$, he calculates an income multiplier for changes in public expenditure of 1.74. Using exactly the same structural equations and data, he derives a coefficient based on the alternate definition, $\frac{1}{\delta x_j/\delta y_i}$, of 6.7. The paradox is resolved by considering the economic meaning of the two definitions of "effectiveness" in this case. The multiplier $\delta y_i/\delta x_j$ is the change in target i (income in this example) associated with a given change in instrument j, here defined as public expenditures, *when all other instruments are held constant* (a reduced-form coefficient). The expression $\frac{1}{\delta x_j/\delta y_i}$, on the other hand, represents the reciprocal of the change in instrument j that is needed to sustain a given change in target i, *when all other targets are held constant* (the reciprocal of a structural coefficient).

In the Tinbergen example, $\delta y_i/\delta x_j$ is the multiplier for an open economy, since the other target (specifically, the trade balance) is free to vary. Hence, part of the additional expenditure induced by the budget deficit leaks away in the form of increased imports, reducing the impact on domestic output. On the other hand, $\frac{1}{\delta x_j/\delta y_i}$ means that the "other target," the balance of trade, remains unchanged, so that such leakage via an increased deficit or reduced surplus is prohibited by assumption. In a small country like the Netherlands, where the marginal propensity to import is undoubtedly high, it is not at all surprising that the two coefficients should be so different. Which

---

[5] Using the matrix notation of page 3, and ignoring the exogenous disturbance terms for simplicity, $\frac{\delta y_i}{\delta x_j} = b_{ij}$, while $\frac{1}{\delta x_j/\delta y_i} = \frac{|B|}{|B_{ij}|}$, where $|B_{ij}|$ is the cofactor of the "ij-th" element of B and $|B|$ is the determinant of B.

measure is the appropriate one depends, of course, on the context of the problem at hand, but considerable confusion can arise from failure to distinguish between the two.

In addition to the requirement that instruments be effective, a unique solution to the problem of achieving the desired values of the target variables will exist only if the requirements of "Tinbergen's Rule" are fulfilled: *that the number of independent targets must equal the number of independent instruments.*[6]

If there are fewer targets than policy variables, then there are fewer equations than unknowns and the system is underdetermined, that is, there is no unique policy solution, but an infinite number of them. If a country is concerned with, say, achieving only internal balance and can use both monetary and fiscal policy to achieve this goal, there is in principle an infinite number of monetary-fiscal combinations which can be used to reach the desired level of real income.

If on the other hand, there are more targets than policy variables, the system has more equations than unknowns. It will not then, in general, be possible to find a set of values for the policy tools that will satisfy all the equations, that is, that will permit all targets to be achieved. In everyday terminology, this is a situation in which there are not enough tools to do the job.

To illustrate the problems that arise when the number of targets does not equal the number of instruments, or when either some of the instruments or some of the targets are not independent, let us consider a simple two-by-two case in which monetary and fiscal policy, x_1 and x_2, are used to achieve a desired level of income, y_1^*, and a desired balance-of-payments position, y_2^*. A geometrical illustration of the independence requirements can then be given with the aid of Figure 1, below, which is an adaptation of the geometry used by Mundell [22] in one of his best-known articles on the internal-external-balance problem. In Figure 1, II and EE stand for combinations of "monetary policy," represented by the rate of interest, and "fiscal policy," represented by government deficit expenditures, that will yield, respectively, internal and external balance. That is, at every point on II, $dy_1^* = 0$, and at every point on EE, $dy_2^* = 0$. The internal-

---

[6] If this condition is not met, the B matrix will be singular, that is, its determinant will equal zero and the inverse matrix, B^{-1}, required for a solution to the policy problem, will not exist. This criterion applies when the causal relationships are linear and uncertainty is absent. The modifications required by the relaxation of these assumptions will be discussed in a later section.

balance locus (II) has a positive slope because a higher interest rate would reduce income (y_1) if it were not accompanied by a larger government deficit. Similarly, the external-balance locus (EE) has a positive slope, because a higher interest rate would improve the balance of payments (y_2) via both capital inflows and an improved trade balance as income and therefore spending are reduced, unless it were accompanied by an increase in deficit spending by the government.

Figure 1 also depicts four zones of disequilibrium. To the left of EE, the interest rate (x_1) is too low and/or the budget deficit (x_2) is too large, so that the balance of payments is in deficit, whereas the opposite combination causes a surplus to the right of EE. Above II,

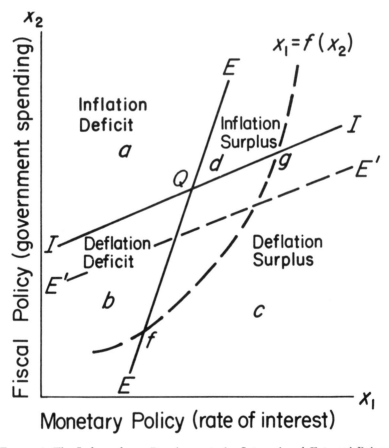

FIGURE 1. The Independence Requirements for Internal and External Balance

6

the combination of policies is too expansionary and inflationary pressure occurs. The reverse is true below II. The letter within each zone indicates the particular type of disequilibrium that characterizes that zone.[7]

With this framework, we are in a position to examine the cases in which the independence required by "Tinbergen's Rule" does not hold, with the result that there does not exist any unique combination of monetary and fiscal policy, such as that represented by point Q in Figure 1, which yields simultaneously both internal and external balance.

First, assume that the two policy instruments are dependent, so that a given level of one implies a particular level of the other; that, for example, any given change in public expenditures implies a particular change in the money supply.[8] If fiscal policy is used, say, to maintain internal balance, then monetary policy is not free to function as required to achieve external balance. For operational purposes, the two instruments have collapsed into one, and the system is one instrument short, a situation depicted in Figure 1 by the line $x_1 = f(x_2)$.[9] This line would intersect EE and II at point Q only fortuitously.

---

[7] Strictly speaking, the regions labelled "inflation" in the diagram must be interpreted as situations of inflationary pressure, with excess demand at full employment prevented from raising prices by some form of rationing device. A situation of dynamic inflation, with continuously changing price levels and expectations, cannot be handled with such a model. In fact, Quirk and Zarley [31] argue that, because it does not take into account the fundamental changes in the working of the economy above the full-employment level, the Mundell-type model is, strictly speaking, applicable only to disequilibrium positions below full employment. They suggest, further, that Mundell's conclusions concerning the stability of a system ensured by the application of his Principle of Effective Market Classification (see Section C, below) are quite sensitive to the assumptions made about the determination of the level of output in disequilibrium states, assumptions which are not spelled out by either Mundell or his followers.

[8] More precisely, a once-over increase in government expenditures to a sustained deficit level implies a continuously increasing money supply. The money supply will increase in each period by an amount equal to the level of (not the increase in) deficit spending by the government. A stable relationship between the level of deficit spending and the interest rate is possible only in an economy which is growing at a rate such that the increasing demand for money exactly matches the increasing supply at an unchanged interest rate. This aspect of the stock-flow problem is evaded by most of the short-run Keynesian models dealing with monetary and fiscal policy.

[9] Actually, we cannot know anything about the nature of the functional relationship between x_1 and x_2, not even whether it is positive or negative, without more information, specifically about the behavioral functions which determine the relationship between changes in the money supply and in the rate of interest. Once these relationships are defined, however, as they are in the model described on pp. 14-15, the functional relationship $x_1 = f(x_2)$ is determined.

In general, both equations could not be satisfied; the economy could reach either external balance at point f in Figure 1 or internal balance at point g, but both targets could not, except by chance, be simultaneously reached.

The two targets in the system will be linearly dependent when the EE locus has the same slope as the II locus, as is the case with $E'E'$ in Figure 1. In economic terms, this means that the relative effectiveness of the two types of policy with respect to changes in the level of domestic income is exactly the same as their relative effectiveness with respect to changes in the balance of payments.

This situation will occur only if monetary policy has no impact on capital flows. For in this case both monetary and fiscal policy will affect the balance of payments in exactly the same way: via a change in the trade balance which is equal in each case to the induced change in income multiplied by the marginal propensity to import (on the usual Keynesian assumption that exports are exogenously determined). If, on the other hand, international capital flows have any interest elasticity at all, the relative effectiveness of the two instruments in terms of internal balance will remain unchanged, but monetary policy will now have an additional effect on the balance of payments through the international flow of capital which results from a change in the rate of interest, here taken as the monetary-policy variable. This additional effect increases the relative effectivenses of monetary as compared with fiscal policy in achieving external balance, making EE steeper than II.[10]

---

[10] This can be shown algebraically by writing out the equations for the internal and external balance lines, respectively (holding the exogenous w terms constant), as:

(1a) $$dy_1{}^* = b_{11}\, dx_1 + b_{12}\, dx_2 = 0 = \frac{\delta y_1{}^*}{\delta x_1}\, dx_1 + \frac{\delta y_1{}^*}{\delta x_2}\, dx_2;$$

(1b) $$dy_2{}^* = b_{21}\, dx_1 + b_{22}\, dx_2 = 0 = \frac{\delta y_2{}^*}{\delta x_1}\, dx_1 + \frac{\delta y_2{}^*}{\delta x_2}\, dx_2.$$

Solving these expressions for the slope of II, $(dx_2/dx_1)_{II}$, and the slope of EE, $(dx_2/dx_1)_{EE}$, we have:

(1c) $(dx_2/dx_1)_{II} = -\dfrac{\delta y_1/\delta x_1}{\delta y_1/\delta x_2};$ (1d) $(dx_2/dx_1)_{EE} = -\dfrac{\delta y_2/\delta x_1}{\delta y_2/\delta x_2}.$

The denominators of these expressions are related via the equation

$$\frac{\delta y_2}{\delta x_2} = -m(\delta y_1/\delta x_2),$$

where m is the marginal propensity to import; the numerators are related via:

There can be no point of intersection, like Q, representing a position of both internal and external balance, when the slopes of EE and II are equal. In general, the internal- and external-balance schedules will be parallel and nonintersecting, like II and $E'E'$, indicating that the two targets are inconsistent, since there is no possible combination of monetary and fiscal policies which can yield both internal and external balance.[11] If, on the other hand, we have the special case in which the exogenously determined w variables happen to take on values which shift II so as to coincide with $E'E'$, then there is an infinite number of solutions to the system; the targets are for operational purposes one and the same. Implicit in this example is an important point: targets are dependent or independent only with respect to a particular set of instruments; in the example just given, the substitution of a new instrument for one of the original ones could change the slope of one or both of the balance lines and thus create independence among targets which did not exist before.

In summary, Tinbergen's Rule says that, within the framework of the linear fixed-targets model, a unique combination of policy tools consistent with the achievement of both internal and external balance cannot exist unless the number of independent policy instruments available is the same as the number of independent economic objectives (targets) toward which these policies are directed. If the number of instruments does not equal the number of targets, the system will be either over- or under-determined; there will be either no solution or an infinite number of them. If the number of targets equals the

---

$\frac{\delta y_2}{\delta x_1} = -m(\delta y_1/\delta x_1) + (\delta K/\delta x_1)$, where K is the net inflow of capital. If we substitute these last two expressions into (1d), we obtain the following relationship between the slopes of EE and II:

(1e) $\quad (dx_2/dx_1)_{EE} = \dfrac{-m(\delta y_1/\delta x_1) + (\delta K/\delta x_1)}{m(\delta y_1/\delta x_2)} = -\dfrac{\delta y_1/\delta x_1}{\delta y_1/\delta x_2} + \dfrac{\delta K/\delta x_1}{m(\delta y_1/\delta x_2)}$

$$= \left(\frac{dx_2}{dx_1}\right)_{II} + \frac{\delta K/dx_1}{m\,(\delta y_1/\delta x_2)}.$$

These slopes will be equal if $\delta K/\delta x_1 = 0$; in this case, where $\dfrac{\delta y_1/\delta x_1}{\delta y_1/\delta x_2} = \dfrac{\delta y_2/\delta x_1}{\delta y_2/\delta x_2}$, the Jacobian of the system is singular and its inverse nonexistent, so that no unique solution exists.

[11] The introduction of a third policy instrument, such as commercial policy, could bring about a *shift* in one of the lines, in this case probably the external-balance line, until it coincided with the internal-balance line. This would imply a move from the inconsistent case, where no joint-balance point exists, to the trivial case, where there is an infinite number of such points, since any policy combination leading to internal balance will lead to external balance as well.

number of instruments but two or more targets or policy instruments are not independent, then no solution will exist, except fortuitously.

C. The Principle of Effective Market Classification

In stressing the interdependence of targets and instruments, the model just discussed reflects the fact that an effective instrument of economic policy will generally have an impact on more than one target, and any broad macroeconomic target like full employment or balance-of-payments equilibrium is almost certain to be affected by more than one type of policy action. Nor, in a world of centralized decision-making, complete information, and instantaneous adjustment, would this complex web of interrelationships cause any particular difficulties. As long as the targets were not inconsistent and the government had at hand a sufficient number of independent effective instruments, all the policy variables could be set at the necessary levels and all targets achieved simultaneously, by setting $X^* = B^{-1}Y^*$.

In reality, however, policies affect targets only with lags of varying magnitudes, all targets are never achieved simultaneously, and no country possesses an omniscient and omnipotent central-planning agency, charged with the responsibility for achieving all economic targets and vested with authority to manipulate freely all economic-policy variables. In many countries, different policy instruments are in the hands of different authorities. In the United States, for example, fiscal policy is the joint responsibility of the President and the Congress, whereas monetary policy is the specific domain of the Federal Reserve System. The most casual perusal of the recent history of economic policy-making yields ample evidence of how imperfect is the coordination of these two major policy instruments.

As a guide to the proper assignment of instruments to targets in a world where authority is decentralized and information about the operation of the economic system is always incomplete, Mundell [22] offers a second-best criterion which he terms the Principle of Effective Market Classification (EMC Principle): *that each policy instrument should be directed toward that target on which it has relatively the greatest impact.*[12] To apply this criterion, we must have *a priori* knowledge not only about the *direction* of change of one variable in response to a given change in another but also, obviously, about the *relative* impact of

[12] With consideration of the EMC Principle, we move from the context of comparative statics, where only the characteristics of equilibrium positions are considered, to that of policy dynamics, where the nature of disequilibrium positions

different policy variables on the various target variables, but we need not know the *absolute* magnitudes of these responses.

Mundell's EMC Principle arises from the relationship between the slopes of the lines representing external (*EE*) and internal (*II*) balance in Figure 1. In a system where each policy instrument is assigned the task of trying to achieve one target, the stability of the system depends crucially on these relative slopes.

We have observed earlier (p. 8) that, if international capital flows are at all sensitive to interest-rate differentials between countries, the *EE* curve will be steeper than the *II* curve, indicating that monetary policy is relatively more effective in achieving external balance and fiscal policy, internal balance. This is because fiscal policy operates on the balance of payments only via its effect on income, spending, and imports, whereas monetary policy has, in addition to this same impact, an additional effect on the capital account.

To illustrate the meaning of the EMC Principle, assume that the economy is initially in a situation of disequilibrium illustrated by point *W* in Figure 2, characterized by full employment (internal balance) at home and a deficit in the balance of payments. Note that the arrows emanating from points *a*, *b*, *c*, and *d* indicate the direction that monetary and fiscal policy would take if the economy were experiencing the type of disequilibrium represented by each of these zones. If the proper assignment of policies according to the EMC Principle is made, as indicated by the *solid* arrows in zones *b* and *d*, the rate of interest will be raised until external balance is reached at *S*; this will cause some recession domestically, which is offset by an increase in government deficit spending until internal equilibrium is reached at *T*, and so forth. Clearly this process of fluctuation with

---

and the characteristics of the adjustment path become central to the analysis. In the comparative-statics models, dynamic considerations enter only through the occasional use of the correspondence principle. That is, the assumption that a system is dynamically stable is utilized to deduce certain characteristics of the comparative-statistics system, generally the sign of one or more determinants. (The correspondence principle is developed in P.A. Samuelson, *Foundations of Economic Analysis*, New York, 1965, Chs. 9 and 10.) The purpose of the EMC Principle, on the other hand, is to provide a decision-rule which will ensure dynamic stability. For a mathematical formulation of this Principle and a discussion of its relationship to the conditions required for dynamic stability in the two-target/two-instrument case, see Cooper [4, pp. 8-12] or Mundell [25, pp. 214-216]. Unfortunately, no simple way of generalizing the EMC Principle to the $n \times n$ case has yet been found. For some of the difficulties associated with such a generalization, see Mundell [25, ch. 21] and Kelvin Lancaster, *Mathematical Economics* (New York: 1968), pp. 206-209.

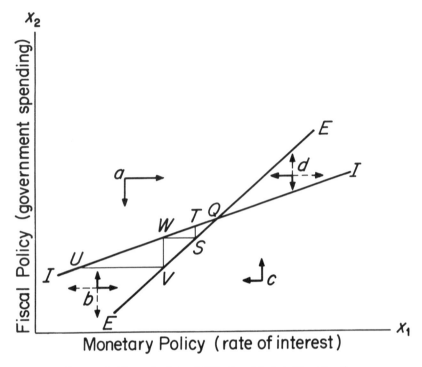

FIGURE 2. The Principle of Effective Market Classification

progressively smaller amplitudes will lead eventually to the internal-external balance point, Q.

Assume, on the other hand, that the EMC Principle is *not* followed, that is, that monetary policy is directed toward internal balance and fiscal policy toward external balance, so that the directions of change in the policy instruments are indicated by the dotted arrows in zones b and d of Figure 2. (Note that both arrows point directly toward the EE and II loci in zones a and c, whichever assignment is made).[13]

[13] These might be termed the "easy" zones, in the sense that in the inflation-deficit zone a, contractionary policies are indicated to move toward both internal and external balance, whereas in the deflation-surplus zone c, expansionary policies are required for both targets. As long as the economy remains in one of these zones,

12

Then, when the economy is in initial disequilibrium at W, government spending will be reduced until external balance is reached at V, then the interest rate will be lowered to offset the domestic recession just caused, so that the system moves to U, and so forth. The system is clearly unstable; it is moving farther and farther away from equilibrium because improper assignment of instruments to targets has resulted in a situation where each step taken by the monetary authorities worsens the situation which fiscal policy must correct, and each change in fiscal policy, in turn, increases the disequilibrium gap with which monetary policy must deal.

In a world where imperfect knowledge or institutional constraints make it impossible to utilize policy tools in a combination that leads directly to the attainment of all targets, the assignment of each tool to that target on which it exerts relatively the greatest influence will guarantee that the policies do not simply frustrate each other. The proper assignment of policies guarantees nothing about how quickly the system is moving toward equilibrium or if, in fact, it will reach it at all before some new disturbance occurs, but only that it is moving in the right direction.

---

either assignment will be stable. Except by mere chance, however, the magnitude of the policy changes required to achieve external balance will not be exactly the same as that needed for internal balance. And if one of these targets is reached before the other, continued application of monetary and fiscal policy in the same direction will move the economy into one of the "hard" zones b or d, in which the assignment question becomes crucial to the stability of the system.

II. SPECIFIC MODELS AND CONCLUSIONS

A. A Simple Keynesian Model: Some Policy Multipliers

A great variety of models, primarily of the short-run Keynesian type, have been used to seek answers to the problems enumerated in the previous section.[14] Since each model employs a slightly different set of structural equations, reflecting different simplifying assumptions about the operation of an economic system, it would be pointless to describe them in detail.[15] Most of them share, however, certain common features. The targets are almost always internal balance (full-employment output) and external balance (balance-of-payments equilibrium or zero change in reserve levels). We shall use a very simple single-country model of this type—a lowest common denominator, so to speak—in order to illustrate the nature of the work in this area.[16]

The model consists of the following system of identities and behavioral relationships.

(1) $Y = E + T + G_0$, where Y is national income, E is domestic expenditure, T is the trade surplus and G is government deficit spending—the fiscal-policy variable—assumed to be equal to zero initially. (Note that this formulation assumes a zero marginal-tax rate.)

(2) $B = T + K$, where B is the balance of payments and K is the net capital inflow.

(3) $M_0 = L$ where M is the stock of money, the monetary-policy variable, and L the stock of money held by the public (on the

[14] See, for example, [5], [11], [22], [23], [29].

[15] For a helpful discussion of some of the more important short-run demand-oriented models, which he analyzes as variants of a very general internal-external-balance model, see Takayama [37].

[16] This model (and the conclusions that follow) is a somewhat modified version of the one employed by Johnson [11]. It differs from the latter primarily in that Johnson makes the additional assumption that international capital flows are responsive not only to changes in the interest rate but also in the level of income, on the assumption that an increase in income leads to an increase in opportunities for profitable investment and a decrease in income to a decrease in such opportunities. This means that increases in income resulting from expansionary policies will have a positive effect on the balance of payments through the capital account in addition to their negative effect through the trade account. If these income effects on the capital account are strong enough to dominate, many of the policy conclusions just cited will be modified or reversed. See, in addition to Johnson, Baggott and Flanders [1], Patrick [29], and Rhomberg [32].

14

assumption that the monetary authority sterilizes the impact of balance-of-payments surpluses or deficits on the money supply).

(4) $E = E(Y,i); 1 > E_y > 0, E_i < 0$
(where i is the rate of interest).

(5) $T = T(Y,r); -E_y < T_y < 0, T_r > 0$
(where r is the domestic price of foreign exchange).

(6) $K = K(i), K_i > 0$
(on the assumption that the foreign interest rate is constant).

(7) $L = L(Y,i); 1 > L_y > 0, L_i < 0.$

The subscripts indicate partial derivatives. Equations (1) through (3) are market-equilibrium conditions, while (4) through (7) specify the behavioral assumptions. When (4)–(7) are substituted into (1)–(3) and the system is then differentiated totally, we obtain:

$$dY = E_y\,dY + E_i\,di + T_y\,dY + T_r\,dr + dG_0;$$
$$dB = T_y\,dY + K_i\,di + \qquad T_r\,dr;$$
$$dM_0 = L_y\,dY + L_i\,di.$$

Rearranged and written in matrix form, this system is:

$$
\begin{bmatrix}
(1 - E_y - T_y) & -E_i & -T_r & 0 \\
-T_y & -K_i & -T_r & 1 \\
L_y & L_i & 0 & 0
\end{bmatrix}
\begin{bmatrix}
dY \\ di \\ dr \\ dB
\end{bmatrix}
=
\begin{bmatrix}
dG_0 \\ 0 \\ dM_0
\end{bmatrix}.
$$

The three-equation system as it stands contains two policy-determined variables—dG and dM—and four dependent variables—dY, di, dr, and dB. To make such a system determinate, one of the dependent variables must be fixed exogenously, rather than remaining unknown. This can be done by setting $dr = 0$ in a fixed-exchange-rate system, or $dB = 0$ in a flexible-rate system, where the balance of payments is always automatically equilibrated by means of exchange-rate variation. Thus, in the fixed-exchange system the third column of the matrix drops out, while the fourth column drops out in the flexible-exchange system.[17] The determinants of the resulting matrices then become:

$$\Delta_{1(dr=0)} = [-L_i(1 - E_y - T_y) - E_iL_y] > 0,$$
$$\Delta_{2(dB=0)} = T_r[L_y(K_i - E_i) - L_i(1 - E_y)] > 0.$$

[17] In using the real trade balance, T, rather than its domestic-currency value, this model ignores the possible impact of changes in the domestic prices of exports or imports under a system of flexible exchange rates. For this criticism and an alternative formulation, see Sohmen [35]. A corrected version of the Sohmen model is given in Sohmen and Schneeweiss [36].

Now the system is determinate, but it may still be inconsistent; if, with only two policy variables to manipulate, we regard each of the three unknowns as a target variable whose desired level is independently set, one of the target levels will, in the general case, not be met. In most of the policy models under discussion, the problem has been solved by regarding the interest rate not as a target variable but an an "irrelevant" endogenous variable, which is allowed to take on whatever value is required to insure the achievement of the desired values for the true target variables, Y and B (or r).

The system can now be manipulated in a variety of ways. The questions raised by Mundell's EMC Principle concerning the relative efficiency of monetary and fiscal policy in achieving internal and external balance under varying exchange-rate systems have stimulated a good deal of interest in "traditional" solutions which yield policy multipliers: expressions for the effect on each target variable in turn which results from a given change in one of the policy variables when the other policy variables are held unchanged. This approach gives solutions as follows:

(8a) $$\left(\frac{\delta Y}{\delta G}\right)_{(dr=0)} = \frac{-L_i}{\Delta_1} > 0;$$

(8b) $$\left(\frac{\delta B}{\delta G}\right)_{(dr=0)} = \frac{K_i L_y - T_y L_i}{\Delta_1} \gtrless 0;$$

(8c) $$\left(\frac{\delta Y}{\delta M}\right)_{(dr=0)} = \frac{-E_i}{\Delta_1} > 0;$$

(8d) $$\left(\frac{\delta B}{\delta M}\right)_{(dr=0)} = \frac{-K_i(1 - E_y - T_y) - E_i T_y}{\Delta_1} < 0;$$

(9a) $$\left(\frac{\delta Y}{\delta G}\right)_{(dB=0)} = \frac{-L_i T_r}{\Delta_2} > 0;$$

(9b) $$\left(\frac{\delta r}{\delta G}\right)_{(dB=0)} = \frac{K_i L_y - T_y L_i}{\Delta_2} \gtrless 0;$$

(9c) $$\left(\frac{\delta Y}{\delta M}\right)_{(dB=0)} = \frac{T_r(K_i - E_i)}{\Delta_2} > 0;$$

(9d) $$\left(\frac{\delta r}{\delta M}\right)_{(dB=0)} = \frac{K_i(1 - E_y - T_y) + T_y E_i}{\Delta_2} > 0.$$

In all but two cases, the signs of the policy multipliers are known for certain. In general, an increase in the money supply will increase income and worsen the balance of payments (or depreciate the home currency in a flexible system). An increase in deficit spending will

16

raise income under both exchange systems, but it may worsen or improve the balance of payments (or the value of the home currency when $dB = 0$), depending on which of two conflicting forces dominates: the negative impact of the increase in income and expenditures on the trade balance, or the capital inflow attracted by the rise in the interest rate due to an increase in expenditures with the money supply held fixed. The net effect depends on the sign of the term $(K_i L_y - T_y L_i)$ in equations (8b) and (9b). When capital movements are very interest-elastic, so that K_i is high, this term will be dominated by $K_i L_y$, and the higher G and i will improve the balance of payments by attracting large inflows of capital. The reverse will be true when capital flows are interest-inelastic.

In the latter case, when $K_i L_y < T_y L_i$, implying that an increase in G will lead to a net deterioration in the balance of payments or the exchange rate, Mundell's assignment of monetary policy to external and fiscal policy to internal balance under the EMC Principle still holds under both the fixed- and the flexible-exchange-rate systems. To show this, we compute the slopes of the external- and internal-balance lines as follows:

$$(10a) \quad \left(\frac{dG}{dM} \right)_{II(dr=0)} = - \frac{\frac{\delta Y}{\delta M}}{\frac{\delta Y}{\delta G}} = \frac{-E_i}{L_i}.$$

$$(10b) \quad \left(\frac{dG}{dM} \right)_{EE(dr=0)} = - \frac{\frac{\delta B}{\delta M}}{\frac{\delta B}{\delta G}} = \frac{K_i(1 - E_y - T_y) + E_i T_y}{K_i L_y - T_y L_i}.$$

$$(11a) \quad \left(\frac{dG}{dM} \right)_{II(dB=0)} = \frac{K_i - E_i}{L_i}.$$

$$(11b) \quad \left(\frac{dG}{dM} \right)_{EE(dB=0)} = \frac{K_i(1 - E_y - T_y) + E_i T_y}{K_i L_y - T_y L_i}.$$

If $K_i L_y < T_y L_i$, all four of these expressions are negative, and one can show quite simply that $\left| \left(\frac{dG}{dM} \right)_{II} \right| < \left| \left(\frac{dG}{dM} \right)_{EE} \right|$ under either fixed or flexible exchange rates as long as $K_i > 0$.[18] If $K_i L_y > T_y L_i$, implying that EE is upward rather than downward sloping, so that an increase

---

[18] The exact conditions are, for the fixed-exchange-rate case $(dr = 0)$: $K_i[L_i(1 - E_y - T_y) + E_i L_y] < 0$; for the flexible-exchange-rate case $(dB = 0)$: $K_i[E_i L_y - L_y K_i + L_i K_i(1 - E_y)] < 0$.

17

in deficit spending must be accompanied by an *increase* in the money supply in order to maintain external balance, *either* assignment is in fact stable, regardless of the relative effectiveness of the two instruments.[19] Thus, the instability problem which the EMC criterion was designed to solve could not arise in this case and knowledge of the sign of $(K_iL_y - T_yL_i)$ is unnecessary; assignment of monetary policy to external and fiscal policy to internal balance would insure stability in either case.

The multipliers of (8) and (9) can also be used to answer a wide variety of related questions concerning the impact of a particular policy instrument on a particular target. In some cases, inspection of them will reveal directly that a particular instrument will be more effective in raising income under a flexible- than under a fixed-exchange-rate system. Such is the case, for example, for $\delta Y/\delta M$, which must be larger under the flexible- than under the fixed-exchange-rate system, since $\dfrac{T_r(K_i - E_i)}{\Delta_2} > \dfrac{-E_i}{\Delta_1}.$[20] And, where the general case is ambiguous, we can at least tell under what conditions (that is, for what ranges of the relevant functional relationships) the policy impact will be greater in one case than in the other. For example, the impact of an increase in deficit spending on domestic income will be greater under the fixed- than under the flexible-exchange-rate system:

$$\left[\left(\frac{\delta Y}{\delta G}\right)_{(dr=0)} > \left(\frac{\delta Y}{\delta G}\right)_{(dB=0)} \right],$$

if and only if $K_iL_y > T_yL_i$, that is, under conditions which lead in the fixed-rate case to an improvement in the balance of payments and therefore in the flexible exchange rate to an appreciation of the exhange rate, which will wipe out part of the initial multiplier effect on income by causing a deterioration of the trade balance.

To go any further along these lines, we require some assumptions about the prevailing degree of international capital mobility. If the interest-rate responsiveness of international flows of financial capital is low—in the limit, nonexistent—, both monetary and fiscal policy will have a greater impact on domestic income and employment under

[19] For proof of this stability, see Levin [17]. I am grateful to Professor Levin for calling this implication to my attention.

[20] The reader can easily prove this assertion for himself by writing out Δ_1 and Δ_2, cross-multiplying the resulting ratios, and cancelling terms.

flexible than under fixed exchange rates, that is, when

$$K_i \to 0, \quad \frac{T_r(K_i - E_i)}{\Delta_2} > \frac{-E_i}{\Delta_1} \quad \text{and} \quad \frac{-L_iT_r}{\Delta_2} > \frac{-L_i}{\Delta_1}.^{21}$$

In essence, the reason is that, under a system of fixed exchange rates, a certain proportion of the expansionary stimulus "leaks abroad" through increased imports and the resulting trade deficit, whereas under the system of flexible exchange rates, this leakage will be prevented by an exchange depreciation sufficient to maintain a zero trade balance.[22] Thus, the multiplier will be that for a closed economy, $1/s$ (where s is the marginal propensity to save), rather than the smaller multiplier, $1/s + m$ (where m is the marginal propensity to import), applicable to an open one.

If there is a high degree of international capital mobility, on the other hand, the conclusions are different. To see why, it is simplest to consider the limiting case where the sensitivity of international capital flows to interest-rate differentials is infinite, meaning that interest rates are equalized the world over and that the domestic rate is "frozen" at the world level by the potential inflows or outflows of capital which would result from any pressure to depart from that level.[23]

---

[21] When Δ_1 and Δ_2 are written out, we have

$$\frac{T_r(K_i - E_i)}{T_r[L_y(K_i - E_i) - L_i(1 - E_y)]} > \frac{-E_i}{-L_i(1 - E_y - T_y) - E_iL_y}$$

$$\text{and} \quad \frac{-L_iT_r}{T_r[L_y(K_i - E_i) - L_i(1 - E_y)]} > \frac{-L_i}{-L_i(1 - E_y - T_y) - E_iL_y}.$$

When $K_i \to 0$, these expressions are approximated by:

$$\frac{-E_i}{-L_i(1 - E_y) - L_yE_i} > \frac{-E_i}{-L_i(1 - E_y - T_y) - L_yE_i}$$

$$\text{and} \quad \frac{-L_i}{-L_i(1 - E_y) - L_yE_i} > \frac{-L_i}{-L_i(1 - E_y - T_y) - E_iL_y},$$

both of which hold because $-E_y < T_y < 0$.

[22] When capital flows are absent, a zero balance of payments implies a zero balance of trade.

[23] If we define the monetary instrument as a change in the money supply, as is usually done in models of the type we are describing, the effectiveness of monetary policy in changing the level of domestic income is unaffected by changes in K_i, as (8c) shows, until the limiting case of $K_i \to \infty$, when the mechanism breaks down because the interest rate cannot change. In this case, it becomes clear that the monetary instrument must be redefined. If, however, we employ an operational definition of a truly exogenous monetary-policy variable from the beginning, we can see that an increase in the interest sensitivity of capital flows reduces the internal

19

In this limiting situation, monetary policy is still a more effective stabilizer of domestic income under flexible than under fixed exchange rates, that is, when $K_i \to \infty$, $\dfrac{T_r(K_i - E_i)}{\Delta_2} > \dfrac{-E_i}{\Delta_1}$. Indeed, under the latter system it can have no impact on domestic income at all, since its normal stimulus to investment and perhaps also consumption expenditures via a lowered interest rate is thwarted by the fact that the interest rate cannot change;[24] capital-market integration destroys the independence of monetary policy under fixed exchange rates. Under flexible rates, by contrast, the downward pressure on the domestic interest rate stemming from expansionary monetary policy will cause an outflow of capital (even though the interest rate does not actually change) and a potential payments deficit. The exchange depreciation required to maintain balance will stimulate exports and discourage imports, and the resulting trade surplus will stimulate domestic income and employment.

But now, in contrast to the case of low capital mobility, fiscal policy will be more effective under fixed exchange rates, that is, when $K_i \to \infty$, $\dfrac{-L_i}{\Delta_1} > \dfrac{-L_i T_r}{\Delta_2}$. In fact, fiscal policy will now have no domestic impact at all under the flexible system, that is, $\dfrac{-L_i T_r}{\Delta_2} \to 0$ as $K_i \to \infty$. For, an increase in net government expenditures unaccompanied by any increase in the money supply will put upward pressure

---

effectiveness of monetary policy continuously, and not just in the limiting case.

To see this, drop the implicit sterilization assumption and define the change in the money supply as having a policy-controlled component, dO, the monetary-policy variable, and a reserve-change component, $dR = \int_o^t B$. Then $dM = dO + dR = (1 + dR/dO)dO$. As Sohmen and Schneeweiss [36, pp. 338-39] have shown, $dR/dO = -1$ and, therefore, $dM = 0$; without sterilization of changes in reserves, the equilibrium money supply cannot change, and $\delta Y/\delta O = 0$. Now, the larger is K_i, the larger will be the change in the policy-controlled component of the money-supply, dO, required to achieve a given change in the total money supply, dM, in the face of reserve changes caused by induced capital flows. As $K_i \to \infty$, the change in the monetary-policy variable, dO, required for sterilization also $\to \infty$, so that sterilization becomes impossible and $dM \to 0$.

[24] Under these conditions, an expansionary monetary policy will lead only to a continuing loss of exchange reserves via the capital outflow which maintains the domestic interest rate at the world level. The only logically consistent definition of monetary policy when the interest elasticity of international capital flows is infinite is in terms of open-market operations, since under these conditions the government can control neither the domestic interest rate nor the money supply. See Mundell [23, pp. 481-482], and the preceding footnote.

on the rate of interest; the resulting inflow of capital will cause an appreciation of the exchange rate, and the deflationary impact of this appreciation on the trade balance will exactly offset the initial multiplier effect of fiscal policy on domestic income. With a given liquidity-preference schedule and a frozen interest rate, domestic income cannot change without a change in the money supply.

For the in-between situation of less-than-infinite capital mobility, the conclusions follow that monetary policy will always be a more effective instrument for increasing domestic income and employment under flexible than under fixed exchange rates, $(T_r(K_i - E_i)/\Delta_2 > -E_i/\Delta_1$, whatever the value of $K_i)$, whereas fiscal policy will usually be more effective under fixed than under flexible rates (when $K_i L_y > T_y L_i$).

B. The Keynesian Model: Some "Inverted" Solutions

Often more relevant to questions of policy determination are the solutions to the "inverted" form of the system, where one solves for the values of the policy variables required to achieve given levels of the target variables.

In the context of the model we are considering, this means that all dY terms, dB terms, and dr terms are taken as exogenous, while dG terms, di terms, and dM terms are taken as unknowns. In matrix form, the fixed- and flexible-exchange-rate systems become, respectively:

Fixed Exchange Rate (all dr terms are zero):

$$\begin{bmatrix} 1 & E_i & 0 \\ 0 & K_i & 0 \\ 0 & -L_i & 1 \end{bmatrix} \begin{bmatrix} dG \\ di \\ dM \end{bmatrix} = \begin{bmatrix} (1 - E_y - T_y)\,dY \\ dB - T_y\,dY \\ L_y\,dY \end{bmatrix}.$$

Flexible Exchange Rate (all dB terms are zero):

$$\begin{bmatrix} 1 & E_i & 0 \\ 0 & K_i & 0 \\ 0 & -L_i & 1 \end{bmatrix} \begin{bmatrix} dG \\ di \\ dM \end{bmatrix} = \begin{bmatrix} (1 - E_y - T_y)\,dY - T_r\,dr \\ -T_y\,dY - T_r\,dr \\ L_y\,dY \end{bmatrix}.$$

Notice that the basic determinant, Δ_3, is the same under either exchange system:

$$\Delta_3 = K_i > 0,$$

and that it vanishes, so that the system has no unique solution, when capital flows are unresponsive to interest-rate changes.

We can solve either system for dG or dM in terms of dY and either dr or dB.

21

Fixed Exchange Rate:

(12a) $$dG = \left(\frac{K_i(1 - E_y - T_y) + E_iT_y}{\Delta_3}\right) dY - \left(\frac{E_i}{\Delta_3}\right) dB.$$

(12b) $$dM = \left(\frac{K_iL_y - T_yL_i}{\Delta_3}\right) dY + \left(\frac{L_i}{\Delta_3}\right) dB.$$

Flexible Exchange Rate:

(13a) $$dG = \left(\frac{K_i(1 - E_y - T_y) + E_iT_y}{\Delta_3}\right) dY + \left(\frac{T_r(E_i - K_i)}{\Delta_3}\right) dr.$$

(13b) $$dM = \left(\frac{K_iL_y - T_yL_i}{\Delta_3}\right) dY - \left(\frac{T_rL_i}{\Delta_3}\right) dr.$$

The coefficient of each of the target variables represents the direction and relative magnitude of the shift which must take place in the policy variables if the desired change in one target variable is to be achieved while the level of the other target variable remains unchanged. For example, we can tell by inspection of the equations above that, in order to achieve an increase in domestic income with no change in the balance of payments or the exchange rate, a nation should pursue expansionary fiscal policy (the coefficients of dY in the equations for dG are positive, and identical, under both exchange-rate systems). Whether the accompanying monetary policy should be expansionary or contractionary depends, under both systems, on the sign of $(K_iL_y - T_yL_i)$, which represents the difference between the (positive) interest-rate effect and the (negative) income effect on the balance of payments, "weighted" respectively by the transactions demand for money in response to income changes (L_y) and the liquidity-preference response to interest-rate changes (L_i).[25] As we see from equations (8b) and (9b), the sign of this term determines whether the impact of fiscal policy alone would be to cause the balance of payments to improve (the exchange rate to appreciate) or to deteriorate (depreciate). In the first case, the money supply should be increased so as to lower the interest rate and cause capital outflows; in the latter, it should be reduced so as to raise the interest rate and attract capital inflows.

Similarly, when the signs of the partial derivatives are examined, the above equations tell us that, in order to improve the balance of payments or appreciate the exchange rate while maintaining a constant level of domestic income, we should increase government spend-

[25] See Baggott and Flanders [1, p. 6].

ing and reduce the money supply. Both policies will raise the rate of interest (which the reader can verify by solving the system for di) and, by attracting capital inflows, bring about the desired result as income and thus the trade balance remain unchanged.

C. International Capital Movements: Flow versus Stock Models

The Mundell-type model analyzed in the preceding sections has been predicated on the assumption that the international capital flows which take place in response to interest-rate changes are a flow phenomenon, that is, that a one-time change in the level of the interest rate will lead to a steady, permanent inflow or outflow of capital of a given amount per time period. Such an assumption is applicable only in the short run, the period during which the worldwide readjustment of portfolios in terms of the mix of domestic and foreign assets is taking place in response to the changed differential between the domestic and the unchanged foreign interest rate. Once this portfolio-readjustment process is completed, in a nongrowing world with fixed total stocks of assets, the interest-sensitive capital flows will cease.

The opposite view of capital movements is in terms of a stock-adjustment model, whose appropriateness increases as the time horizon lengthens.[26] In terms of this model, the capital movements which take place in response to a change in the interest rate are seen as a transitory phenomenon which cause a once-for-all change in the level of a nation's foreign-exchange reserves, but no change at all in the balance of payments (the time derivative of this reserve stock). The only continuing impact these flows have on the balance of payments is the flow of interest payments to which they give rise, a flow which is universally ignored in flow models, and whose direction of flow is the reverse of that of the capital movements which caused them. In this case, the balance-of-payments equation of (2) becomes,[27]

(14) $\qquad B = T - iA'(i) + i'A(i); \qquad A_i < 0, A_i' > 0,$

where A is the stock of foreign securities held by private domestic residents, A' is the stock of domestic securities held by foreign resi-

---

[26] In Komiya's [15] phraseology, the distinction here is between "impact" and "steady state" effects; between short-run equilibrium, in which the actual surplus or deficit is equal to the ex ante surplus or deficit, and long-run or full equilibrium, in which any such imbalances, implying that asset balances are changing, have been eliminated.

[27] This is the formulation used by Levin [17].

dents, and i' is the foreign interest rate (assumed constant in this one-country model).

The implication of (14) is that an inflow of capital, although it will bring about a once-over increase in the stock of reserves, will cause a deterioration in the balance of payments via the continuing interest payments to which it gives rise; a capital outflow will have just the opposite effects.

We will not repeat for this case the analysis of Sections A and B. But, by substituting equation (14) for (2) and solving the resulting system for policy multipliers corresponding to those of (8) and (9), the reader can verify for himself that, in contrast to the flow model, an increase in government spending will now always cause the balance of payments to deteriorate, and vice versa, while it is the impact of monetary policy whose direction becomes uncertain in this case. Furthermore, derivation of the ratios of relative effectiveness corresponding to (10) verifies what seems intuitively obvious: that in the stock model, in which capital movements have an impact on the balance of payments exactly the opposite of that implied by the flow model, the assignment of instruments to targets implied by the application of the EMC criterion will also be reversed. Furthermore, as Levin [17] has shown, stability can be achieved only if the authorities define the balance-of-payments target in terms of the current account (the trade balance plus net interest flows). No assignment can guarantee stability if the authorities allow themselves to be "distracted" by the transitory flows comprising the capital account and direct one of their policy instruments at the *apparent* overall payments imbalance prevailing at any particular point in time.

In a growing, as opposed to a stationary economy, actual capital flows are likely to be composed of both a stock and a flow component, the former a transitory flow caused by a redistribution of existing assets in response to a change in the interest rate or other relevant parameters, the latter a steady-state equilibrium flow stemming from efforts to achieve the optimum distribution of *new* savings between foreign and domestic assets. Levin [17] combines balance-of-payments equations (2) and (14) to create such a hybrid model, and shows that it yields no unambiguous assignment that can guarantee stability.[28] This is only one of many ambiguities encountered in attempting to

[28] For another analysis which incorporates both the stock and the flow components of capital flows, see Floyd [7].

apply the Tinbergen type of targets-instruments analysis to a model of a growing rather than a stationary economy. Some of these ambiguities will be explored at the end of the next section.

D. Portfolio-Balance Models

In all variants of the model discussed so far, private expenditures have been regarded as a function of income alone. If, however, we take into account the effect on such expenditures of the private stock of wealth as well as of current income, we encounter the "portfolio-balance" requirement: that, in a stationary economy, income cannot be in long-run equilibrium as long as the stock of wealth is changing.

A highly simplified portfolio-balance model, defining long-run equilibrium in a stationary state with home prices and the exchange rate fixed, can be described as follows:

(1) $\quad Y = E + X_0 - I + G_0;$ (6) $\quad E = E[(1 - t)Y, i, W];$

(2) $\quad M_0 = L;$ (7) $\quad I = mY;$

(3) $\quad A = B;$ (8) $\quad L = L[(1 - t)Y, i, W];$

(4) $\quad G_0 - tY = I - X_0;$ (9) $\quad A = A[(1 - t)Y, i, W].$

(5) $\quad W = B + M_0;$

The variables are defined as on pp. 14-15, with the addition of $W =$ the stock of wealth (money plus bonds), $A =$ the net stock of bonds held by the private sector, $B =$ the net supply of bonds available, and $t =$ the proportional-income-tax rate.[29]

The first two equations, defining equilibrium in the commodity and the money markets, are identical to those in the model on page 14, except that the trade surplus is now designated as $(X - I)$, wealth is introduced as an argument in the demand functions, and the tax rate is assumed to be positive, so that the demand for commodities, money, and bonds are functions of *disposable* income. Equation (3) describes bond-market equilibrium, under the assumption that domestic and foreign bonds are perfect substitutes, with B representing the supply of bonds made available by the government and the foreign sector and A the net quantity of bonds the private sector desires to

[29] Note that only three of the equations (1)-(4) are independent. If, for example, the commodity and money markets are in equilibrium—(1), (2), and (4) are satisfied—Walras' Law implies that the bond market must also be in equilibrium. That is, (3) must also be satisfied. Thus, we must drop one of the four to obtain the basic model for solution.

hold.[30] The condition for portfolio-balance in an open economy is represented by equation (4), which says that the government deficit must equal the current-account deficit. This is because a government deficit pumps financial assets into the economy while an excess of imports over exports drains them out; only when the two are equal can the aggregate stock of wealth be unchanging.[31]

For the system of fixed exchange rates, substitution of equation (6) into equation (4) and solution of the resulting differential equation, $dG - tY = mY$, shows the government-spending multiplier to be a function simply of the tax rate and the marginal propensity to import, $dY/dG = 1/t + m$. But such an increase in deficit spending will increase the trade deficit by an equal amount, as is clear from equation (4), a deficit which is financed by the transfer of excess financial assets to foreigners. Monetary policy, on the other hand, whether defined as a change in the money- supply, in the interest rate, or as open market operations, can have no effect whatsoever on the equilibrium level of income. *Because the portfolio-balance requirement is independent of the interest rate, as equation (4) shows, the equilibrium level of output cannot be permanently affected by monetary policy.* An increase in the money supply and the resulting fall in the interest rate will initially stimulate consumption expenditure. But this increased expenditure will lead to increased imports, a deterioration of the trade balance, and a drain of financial assets out of the economy.[32] This reduction of financial assets below the desired level will, in turn, depress expenditures and income until the original level of income is restored and, with it, portfolio balance.

The definition of external or balance-of-payments equilibrium, which was articulated without difficulty for the short-run Keynesian model analyzed earlier, becomes more ambiguous in the context of the portfolio-balance model. This is because the external-balance target

[30] The net quantity held by the private sector is the quantity of bonds issued by the government and by foreigners (the latter may be negative) and held by the private sector. Securities issued by some individuals or corporations in the private sector and held by others will cancel out in the calculation of the aggregate financial holdings of that sector.

[31] Note that capital inflows or outflows do not imply a net gain or loss of financial assets to foreigners. Any such flow involves simply the exchange of one type of financial asset for another.

[32] There is no way the government can offset this loss of financial assets through a negative trade balance except by deficit spending. It could offset the effects on the money supply through sterilization operations but, under fixed exchange rates, such operations maintain a constant money supply only by exchanging bonds for money, so that the total stock of financial assets could not be held constant.

is in a sense automatically fulfilled by the requirement of portfolio balance. For if the asset transfers which finance a surplus or deficit in the balance of trade take place in order to restore the desired level of assets, then they must by definition be "autonomous" and therefore consistent with balance-of-payments equilibrium. If all trade imbalances are financed in the private sector, there is no need for the stock of international reserves held by the government to change and, if the balance-of-payments target is defined in this way, it is self-fulfilling. If, on the other hand, the external target is defined as trade balance, there is no way that the government can achieve this target and at the same time bring about policy-induced changes in the level of domestic income.

All this is from the viewpoint of a single country, however. Persistent capital flows, such as those required for the operation of the government-spending multiplier, described above, are consistent with long-run equilibrium under only one of the following assumptions: (a) that the portfolio-balance requirement (that the total stock of wealth be unchanging in stationary-state equilibrium) is not met in the rest of the world, or (b) that the country in question is so small that any impact its activities have on the asset holdings of the rest of the world can be safely ignored.[33] The analysis of the portfolio-balance model will be carried out first under the assumption that one or the other of these assumptions is met; then we will show what happens when they are dropped, making persistent capital flows of any kind inconsistent with equilibrium.

In order to examine the impact of fiscal and monetary policy on the equilibrium level of domestic income under flexible exchange rates, some modifications of the equation system (1)-(9), above, are required. Two new variables are required: r, the foreign-exchange rate, and K, the net capital inflow, along with three additional equations:[34]

(10) $\quad I - X = K$, the foreign-exchange market-clearing equation;

(11) $\quad\quad K = K(i)$;

(12) $\quad\quad X = X(r)$.

[33] The analysis of this case follows closely that of Oates [27] and McKinnon and Oates [20].

[34] The addition of three equations and only two variables might seem to over-determine the system. Note however that the level of exports, X, which was exogenous in the fixed-exchange-rate case becomes endogenously determined under flexible rates, and is thus the third additional variable required for a just-determined system.

In addition, equation (6) must be replaced by

(6') $I = I(Y,r)$, where $I_Y = m$.

The impact of a change in government expenditures on the level of domestic income in this model depends crucially on the degree of interest responsiveness of international capital flows, K_i. When there is no such capital mobility $(K_i = 0)$, $K = 0$ and equation (10) requires that the current-account balance must be zero in equilibrium; the rise in imports induced by the initial expansion of spending stemming from increased government expenditures will cause a depreciation of the exchange rate and a consequent increase in exports until trade is again balanced. By equation (4), therefore, $G - tY$ must equal zero in the new equilibrium as well as the old; domestic income will rise to the point where the increase in government spending is matched by increased tax revenues; the fiscal-policy multiplier is $1/t$, as it would be in a closed economy.[35]

At the opposite extreme of perfect capital mobility $(K_i = \infty)$, an increase in deficit spending unaccompanied by any increase in the money supply cannot affect the equilibrium level of domestic income for precisely the same reasons as were given on pages 20-21 in the analysis of the short-run Keynesian model. Equation (8) tells us that, when the interest rate is frozen at the world level by perfect capital mobility, no increase in the equilibrium level of income is possible without an increase in the money supply. The deficit-spending multiplier is zero in this case. For values of K_i between 0 and ∞, the values of the deficit-spending multiplier vary between $1/t$ and zero, decreasing continuously as K_i increases.

Under the assumption that the rest of the world adjusts passively to the portfolio-balance requirements of the country in question, monetary policy will have a powerful impact on the level of domestic income under flexible exchange rates. An increase in the stock of money via open-market purchases, for example, will cause a fall in the interest rate, stimulating domestic spending and also causing a capital outflow, and thus a rise in K, which will stimulate exports and discourage imports, leading to a rise in domestic income. This trade

[35] We see now why our earlier assumption (on page 14) of a zero marginal-tax rate had to be dropped in the portfolio-balance system. Without a positive marginal-tax rate, the fiscal-policy multiplier under a system of flexible exchange rates would be infinite.

surplus must be temporary, however, if the equilibrium requirements of equation (4) are to be met; it will fall as imports increase along with money income and will vanish entirely at the new equilibrium level of income. Note, however, that the movement to a higher equilibrium level of income entails a rise also in the equilibrium level of r, the price of foreign exchange. The maintenance of external balance, defined in terms of an unchanged r, is incompatible with policy-induced changes in the level of domestic income. Setting $r = r_0$ will create an over-determined system which has no solution.

If we now drop the assumption of passive adjustment in the rest of the world, and assume explicitly that foreign as well as domestic wealth must be constant in long-run stationary-state equilibrium, we find that monetary policy cannot permanently alter the level of domestic income under flexible exchange rates either. For now all capital flows must be zero in full portfolio-balance equilibrium.[36] An increase in the money supply will still lead initially to a reduction in interest rates, with all the attendant stimulating effects described in the previous paragraph. But, once the stock adjustment of portfolio mixes of domestic and foreign assets has been accomplished, the capital flows will cease and the exchange rate will move to restore current-account balance. Now, however, as long as income and there-fore taxes are above their initial equilibrium level, there will be a government surplus $(G < tY)$, and the resulting drain on private holdings of financial assets will push equilibrium income back to its original level. The requirement that capital flows be zero in equilib-rium implies, in fact, that neither monetary nor fiscal policy can have any impact on the equilibrium level of domestic income under either exchange-rate regime. We leave it to the reader to work out why this is so in specific cases. As a general proof, we need only note that the requirement that $K = 0$ adds one more equation to the system (1)-(12). With the same number of unknowns as before, this additional equation overdetermines the system and thus permits of no solution.

The highly restrictive conclusions reached through the portfolio-balance model stem from wedding the requirements of long-run stock-and-flow equilibrium (as opposed to the short-run flow equilib-rium of the Keynesian model analyzed earlier) to the assumption of a

[36] The assumption of a persistent inflow or outflow of capital at a given domestic interest rate implies that foreigners will continue to exchange bonds for money indefinitely with no change in their rate of interest.

stationary state. When we substitute the assumptions of a growing economy for those of a stationary one by introducing the possibility of equilibrium growth of capacity and output into the model, much of the determinism of the portfolio-balance model disappears. So much of it disappears, in fact, that the derivation of qualitative conclusions in the general case becomes very difficult, as is indicated by Niehans' [26] investigation of the problem of internal-external-balance policy in the context of a simple balanced-growth model. He examines the impact of the level of taxation, t (the fiscal-policy variable), and the ratio of government debt to disposable income, b (the long-run counterpart of open-market operations), on real income and the gold-reserve ratio. Despite the simplicity of the model, in which international capital movements are ruled out, it turns out that one cannot derive general answers either to the "traditional" question—how does a change in the tax rate or in the debt ratio affect real income or the gold-reserve ratio?—or to its "inverted" form—what combinations of tax rates and debt ratios are required to obtain a given level of output or a given gold-reserve ratio?[37] Knowledge of the direction in which every dependent variable is affected by its arguments (that is, knowledge about the signs of all the partial derivatives) is not enough; we also need information about the size, or at least the range, of the various parameters. The analysis undertaken so far suggests that, when the problem is considered in the context of economic growth, one cannot derive general rules about the optimal combination of monetary and fiscal policies in an open economy; there is no such easy escape from the need for specific quantitative knowledge about the structure of the economy in question.

[37] Niehans notes [26, p. 905] that these uncertainties exist independently of the nonlinearities of his model; that is, they arise even when a zero base (a situation without any government activity) is taken as the point of departure for analysis.

III. EXTENSIONS AND QUALIFICATIONS

The purpose of this chapter is two-fold: to discuss some of the qualifications, ambiguities, and unsolved problems surrounding the targets-instruments approach to the formulation of policy models, and to reflect the flavor of recent attempts to refine the internal-external-balance models outlined in the previous sections. We will make no attempt to describe the contribution of each author; rather, we will outline the main issues classified into four broad categories: Problems of Definition, Constraints on Policy Instruments, Speeds of Adjustment, and The Role of Uncertainty.

A. Problems of Definition: Targets, Instruments, and Equilibrium

It may be useful to begin a discussion about the difficulties of definition with the reminder that the ubiquitous distinction between "targets" and "instruments" is quite arbitrary. It is, in fact, a characteristic, and a limitation, of the fixed-targets approach only; a flexible-targets approach requires no such dichotomous categorization of the arguments of the welfare function. One perceptive analyst has argued that "targets" refer to variables about which we care, "instruments" to those about which we do not care.[38] But we can make this distinction only by ignoring the welfare implications inherent in policy-instrument variables themselves, in the form of administrative costs, of costs associated with the misallocation of resources, and of effects on the distribution of income.[39]

Since there are no hard-and-fast rules to determine which variables we care about, nor to spell out the criteria for satisfaction, it is not surprising that no two builders of internal-external-balance models have defined their targets in quite the same way. But considerable confusion has arisen from their common failure to spell out the assumptions implicit in their definitions.[40] In some cases "internal balance"

[38] J. J. Polak, "International Coordination of Economic Policy," IMF *Staff Papers*, IX (July 1962), p. 151, quoted in Mundell [25, p. 202.]

[39] For example, Cooper [3] has pointed out that, since lower interest rates foster higher growth rates, the rate of interest can be regarded as a target rather than an instrument in growth models, serving as a proxy for the rate of growth in the same way that income serves as a proxy for the level of employment in static-equilibrium models. In addition, Johnson [12] points out that the capital flows resulting from policies to achieve external balance are likely to have important welfare effects through their impact in the international distribution of investment resources.

[40] For an excellent discussion of various formulations of economic goals, see Mundell [25, pp. 204-207].

seems to be defined in terms of full employment and domestic price stability, whereas in others it is defined in terms of full employment alone. Is the former in reality a single target or two separate ones or, as Phillips-curve analysis suggests, two incompatible goals? If the latter is the case, how does the policy-maker determine the optimum trade-off point? And even if full employment with price stability is both possible and desirable in a closed economy, it need not be either in an open economy, where the price behavior consistent with the maintenance of external balance is defined in terms of comparative rates of inflation among countries.[41]

The concept of "external balance" is similarly fraught with ambiguities. Are policy-makers really concerned with flow equilibrium, with the maintenance of equality between certain arbitrarily defined categories of international receipts and payments, or are they concerned with the levels of international reserve holdings, or with the rate at which these stocks are changing? And do they perceive the probable implications of inconsistent balance-of-payments targets; what will happen if all countries together are trying to increase their stocks of international reserves faster than the world's supply of gold—the international reserve medium—is growing?[42] Such ambiguities, and many others like them, lie hidden in all the models we have been discussing.

The confusion and ambiguity surrounding the definition of targets is matched by the confusion and ambiguity surrounding the definition of instruments. Some authors define "monetary policy" as control over the interest rate, others as control over the money supply, usually with but sometimes without sterilization of changes in foreign-exchange reserves.[43] Still others, recognizing that neither of these is fully exog-

[41] General price stability is virtually impossible in an open economy because the prices of imported goods, over which the government can have no control, will enter into the determination of the general price level. If, alternatively, price stability is defined in terms of an index of home-produced goods only, the achievement of this target by all countries would mean, under a system of fixed exchange rates, a total paralysis of the international price mechanism; relative price changes among countries would be impossible. See Mundell [25, p. 207].

[42] Patrick [29] demonstrates that if balance-of-payments targets are inconsistent, the achievement of both internal and external equilibrium will be impossible, whatever the assignment of targets to instruments.

[43] Among the alternative models of internal-external balance worked through by Helliwell [9] are two which differ only in that one assumes complete sterilization of the impact of changes in reserves on the money supply and the other no sterilization at all, showing the crucial importance of this particular assumption for the results derived by Mundell and others.

enous and independent of the fiscal-policy variable, define monetary policy simply as open-market operations, with both the interest rate and the money supply determined endogenously.[44] The most common definition of "fiscal policy," in terms of a change in the level of deficit spending by governments with no change in tax rates, is viable only under the peculiar assumption that marginal tax rates are zero. Otherwise, the level of deficit spending will not be wholly exogenous, since the amount of taxes collected will depend on the level of income.

Jones [13] and Ott and Ott [28] have shown that, when some of the structural relationships in the Keynesian model are disaggregated, the particular definition of the policy instrument used may significantly affect the conclusions. Specifically, when one assumes that the marginal propensities to import out of consumption, investment, and government expenditures are different, it turns out that: (a) the impact of fiscal policy defined as changes in government purchases may be quite different from the impact of fiscal policy defined as changes in tax rates and,[45] (b) that the application of the EMC criterion for the pairing of instruments and targets is highly sensitive to the marginal-import propensities associated with consumption, investment, and government spending, as well as to the responsiveness of international capital flows to changes in interest rates.

Jones [13] has attempted to sort out some of the difficulties associated with the definition of instruments and the distinction between instruments and targets. He has developed a two-stage analysis of the problem of static internal-external balance, in which he defines not only targets (the level of income and the balance of payments) and "fundamental" policy instruments (the quantity of money and the level of government expenditures), but also a set of "intermediate" policy variables (aggregate demand and the interest rate) which are

[44] As was pointed out in footnote 24, above, the interest rate and the money supply must be determined endogenously in a system of fixed exchange rates when capital is perfectly mobile internationally. Furthermore, even without capital mobility, changes in the interest rate are not independent of changes in deficit spending. In a pair of unpublished papers written for Professor Robert Stern at the University of Michigan, Marion Nobel and David Richardson have demonstrated that the Mundell assignment according to the EMC Principle still holds when "monetary policy" and "fiscal policy" are redefined as the shifting of the LM and the IS curves, respectively.

[45] When the possibility of changes in tax rates as well as in the level of government spending is introduced into the definition of fiscal policy, demand functions must be defined in terms of disposable income, net of taxes, rather than in terms of income itself.

neither ultimate targets nor directly controllable instruments. The price of this increased clarity in definition is a reduction in the number of instances in which one can derive simple decision rules about the impact of fundamental policy variables on ultimate target variables on the basis of qualitative information alone.[46]

Finally, it is important to keep straight the various meanings of "equilibrium" implicit in the literature on internal-external balance. Equilibrium in a simple Keynesian model means simply that *ex ante* supply equals *ex ante* demand in the money and product markets. Nothing is implied about the level of income or of the balance of payments at such an equilibrium point; it may be characterized by unemployment and a payments surplus or deficit. A position of equilibrium is not necessarily or even generally a position of balance in the sense described earlier, and the term "balance-of-payments equilibrium" can be misleading.

As the formal literature on the targets-instruments problem has broadened from comparative-statics analysis to the policy-oriented dynamics of the EMC Principle, however, there has been a crucial, if implicit, shift in the definition of equilibrium employed. Now equilibrium has become synonymous with a position of internal and external balance; the equilibrium values of targets are now their desired values and, by extension, the equilibrium values of any non-target endogenous variables must be those consistent with the attainment of the desired values of the targets. Machlup [18] has suggested that this introduction of value judgments into the previously scientific term "equilibrium" is unfortunate. Be that as it may, one must be careful to inquire just how different authors are using this term.

B. Constraints on Policy-Variable Magnitudes

One obvious problem stems from the fact that policy variables are generally constrained within certain limits. In any particular situation

[46] In the field of monetary economics, these three levels of variables have been expanded to four: (1) goal variables, which may be observable only with a considerable lag, such as the level of aggregate demand; (2) policy instruments, such as the constellation of actions generally termed "monetary policy"; (3) target variables, which are readily observable, rapidly affected by the policy instrument, and closely related to the goal variable, such as the interest rate in this particular example; and (4) indicators, which enable us to distinguish between exogenous (uncontrolled) and policy-induced changes in the target variable. The monetary base or the "neutralized" money stock is often suggested as the appropriate indicator for relating monetary policy to the level of aggregate demand. For an excellent exposition of this approach, see Saving [34].

there are boundary conditions, some technical (e.g., prices cannot be negative), some institutional (e.g., money wage rates cannot be reduced), some political (e.g., the average tax rate cannot exceed 30 per cent), which limit the range of variation of the policy variables. None of these conditions can be violated in any feasible solution to a policy problem; if one or more of them is violated in the initial solution, they may have to be introduced explicitly into the system as additional targets, and additional instruments brought in to make the simultaneous achievement of all targets possible.[47]

An important paper by Krueger [16], which incorporates most of the conclusions discussed in sections A and B of Chapter II as special cases, emphasizes that such constraints are a major handicap in achieving full internal and external balance. In this model, both exports and the domestic price level are endogenously determined, the possibility of a trade-off between increases in real income and in the price level is taken explicitly into account, and a change in the level of deficit spending by the government can be effected through either a change in the supply of money or the supply of bonds or some combination of the two.

In addition to reproducing all the standard conclusions and pointing out many important assumptions implicit in previous work, the Krueger model generates two broad conclusions: under fixed exchange rates, any level of real income can be achieved without deterioration in the balance of payments as long as international capital flows respond to interest-rate differentials; and, under a flexible-exchange standard, monetary policy alone can be used to attain any desired level of real income if the country is willing to accept fluctuations in the exchange rate.[48] Unfortunately this happy state of affairs dis-

---

[47] I say "may" rather than "will," because one cannot tell in advance what will happen when a violated boundary condition is introduced explicitly into the system as an additional target. It is possible that such a change may lead in turn to the violation of some other boundary condition which originally was satisfied; on the other hand, it is possible that when one of two boundary conditions originally violated is introduced explicitly, the new solution will satisfy the other as well. (Tinbergen [39, p. 44].) The technique of linear programming represents a method of systematizing this trial-and-error process.

[48] On the assumption that real income is determined by the level of aggregate demand, that is, that there are no constraints on the supply side. Helliwell [9, pp 39-41], points out, however, that when both the exchange rate and the level of reserves are incorporated as constraints into the model," there is (at most) only a single monetary and fiscal policy combination which will satisfy the equations of the model and also achieve a particular target income."

appears when limits or boundary conditions are imposed on any variables. For example, real income may not be able to rise to the full-employment level without a deterioration in the balance of payments unless the interest rate rises above some maximum value, say 10 per cent.

As a second example of the problems posed for the application of the EMC Principle by constraints on the values of policy instruments, we have Ott and Ott's [28] simulation of a model of monetary and fiscal-policy adjustment for the United States in recent years. They estimate that, on the assumption that policies were assigned to targets according to the EMC prescription, a short-term interest rate of 7.5 per cent and a tax cut of \$18-21 billion would have been required to restore internal and external balance in 1966. Both these magnitudes, they suggest, might well have proven unacceptable.

C. Speeds of Adjustment

The EMC criterion for the proper pairing of targets and instruments is formulated without incorporating lags, and itself provides no information about the speed of adjustment of the system, the length of time required for the system to come within some designated neighborhood of equilibrium after a disturbance of a particular type and magnitude. Cooper [4] has suggested that application of the EMC Principle will generally maximize the speed of adjustment by minimizing the interactions and feedbacks among policy tools and targets other than the ones with which they are paired.[49] He employs a simple simulation model [3] to support the hypothesis that the larger are these interactions, the longer is the time spent away from equilibrium in an economy that uses a decentralized or uncoordinated approach to policy-making.

But quantitative estimates of the length of time actually required to come within a certain distance of equilibrium would require detailed knowledge about the disturbances, structure, and parameters of a specific model. Few econometric studies of this type have been attempted. A major one is Rhomberg's model of the Canadian economy [32], which seemed to confirm the hypothesis that fiscal policy has a relatively greater impact on domestic income and employment under

---

[49] Cooper's point is that the adjustment-time will generally be shorter the larger is the smallest characteristic root of the B matrix, and that this root will be larger the larger are the diagonal elements of the matrix relative to the off-diagonal ones.

fixed exchange rates and that monetary policy is more effective under flexible rates.[50] However, the time path of approach to equilibrium appears to be rather long; Rhomberg's simulations suggested that it may take 8 to 12 years for policy changes to exert 80 per cent of their ultimate (equilibrium) influence on the dependent variables and that, furthermore, the system appears to approach equilibrium by damped oscillatory cycles rather than directly.

Lack of systematic knowledge about the various time lags in an economic system makes estimation of the time path of the approach to equilibrium difficult; even more important, the widespread failure to incorporate lags into theoretical models of the type under discussion has obscured important questions concerning the stability of target-instruments systems, including those which meet the EMC criterion. Mundell has several times noted in passing [25, chs. 11, 15, 17] that the relative speed with which target variables respond to changes in policy variables may affect the stability characteristics of his models. And, in fact, the effect of incorporating lags of varying length in their responses of policy variables to deviations in the target variables from their desired values or in the responses of target variables to changes in the policy variables, or both, may well be to call in question any generalization whatsoever. Roper [33] has recently shown, for example, that Cooper's conclusion about the speed of adjustment, cited in the first paragraph of this chapter, depends very heavily on his implicit assumption about the lag with which the monetary authorities sterilize the impact of payments imbalances on the domestic money supply. The explicit incorporation of lag structures into targets-instruments models is one of the most urgent requirements for significant progress in this type of analysis.

D. The Role of Uncertainty

The problem of uncertainty in models of internal-external-balance policy has two major aspects. The first is the uncertainty which inevitably surrounds any estimates of the quantitative effects of instruments on targets. Cooper [4] suggests that this can be introduced formally into the model by including a stochastic element in the

---

[50] More recently, Prachowny [30] has estimated the impact of a particular monetary-fiscal policy mix on the GNP and balance of payments of the United States via a 32-equation econometric model. His results again appear to confirm the Mundell proposition, but he does not estimate the time path of approach to equilibrium.

structural relationships (the coefficients of the B matrix). With the introduction of this complication, he points out, one cannot be sure of achieving the desired values of the target variables even if there is a sufficient number of policy instruments available and boundary conditions are not a problem.[51] How, in such a situation, does one choose the optimum values for the policy instruments? Cooper suggests that one reasonable criterion is that the government would want to minimize the variance of each y around its target value y^*, to insure that the "margin of error" around y^* is as small as possible.

It has been shown by Brainard [2] that the way to do this is to direct at a single target, not a single policy instrument, but that combination of *all* the policy instruments which has the smallest coefficient of variation. When there is correlation among the various instruments, or when we generalize to the case of more than one target, the criteria become complex, but one implication of introducing uncertainty is quite general: "since all policy instruments would be used in pursuit of a single target, improvement in performance vis à vis one objective requires sacrificing other objectives—even when the number of instruments exceeds the number of objectives." [2, p. 42.] Once uncertainty is introduced, having an equal number of instruments and targets is no longer sufficient to insure the achievement of all targets. Furthermore, the decentralization of decision-making by assigning specific instruments to specific targets will now not only slow down the approach to the target values, but will also increase the average size of the gap between the desired levels of the target variables and the actual levels that are ultimately reached. Finally, the Brainard prescription is implicitly predicated on one of two assumptions: (1) that there are no administrative, allocative, or distributional costs associated with the use of policy instruments, or (2) that such costs are identical for all combinations of one or more policy instruments which carry the same probability of moving the economy from its initial position to within a specified neighborhood of the target value.

The second aspect of uncertainty arises from the fact that no country exists in a vacuum; other countries are bound to react to and thereby deflect the policy actions of the domestic authorities, thus increasing the unpredictability of the final outcome. Meade's original

[51] The same problem will arise if there is variability in the disturbances, that is, in the A matrix of p. 3. See Cooper [4, p. A-18].

formulation of the problem of internal-external balance was for a two-country world, but most of the subsequent extensions and formalizations of the targets-instruments problem took the form of single-country models.[52] Such models rest on the implicit assumption either that the country in question is too small for its policy actions to have a significant impact on other countries or, alternatively, that its decision-makers are unaware of the possible repercussions from the disturbances transmitted to other countries and their responses.

This single-country approach suppresses the fact that, in a Mundell-type flow model, it is not really changes in the level of domestic interest rates that cause international flows of interest-sensitive capital, but rather changes in the differential between domestic and foreign rates. When a country uses monetary policy to improve its balance of payments by a capital inflow, according to the Mundell prescription, the corresponding capital outflows from other countries will tend to cause a deterioration in their payments balances. If they respond by raising their own interest rates, the impact of monetary policy in the initiating country will be at least partially offset.[53]

Like the use of monetary policy to achieve external balance in a world of fixed exchange rates, the use of such policies to achieve internal balance in a world of flexible exchange rates and interest-responsive capital flows will have a disturbing impact on foreign income levels. Expansionary monetary policy achieves its efficacy for internal-balance targets in this situation by causing a capital outflow, a depreciation of the exchange rate, and a resulting surplus in the current-account balance which stimulates domestic income and output. But these changes must inevitably be accompanied by appreciating exchange rates and current-account deficits in other countries which will exert a depressing impact on their economies. A country which expands its domestic income and output by this means is doing so by exporting depression to other countries. Krueger [16] points out that this impact, and the responses of countries determined to maintain domestic or external targets of their own, represents a

[52] Patrick [29] is an exception. He analyzes a two-country model, assuming first passive and then active responses on the part of the second country, concluding that the assignment of policies according to the EMC Principle remains stable *unless* interest rates in the two countries are functionally linked to each other.

[53] Patrick points out that in such circumstances, a point may be reached "where interest rates have a more powerful influence on income than on the balance of payments, compared to fiscal policy. At this point, the Mundell assignment becomes inappropriate." [29, p. 280.]

serious qualification to the conclusion implied by her generalized version of the single-country Mundell model: that in a world of flexible exchange rates and interest-responsive capital flows, a country can expand domestic income simply by increasing its money supply.

More generally, Kemp [14] has shown, utilizing a model even simpler than the one developed on pages 14-15 here but incorporating two countries, that the use of monetary and fiscal policy in a system of fixed exchange rates will have disturbing effects on foreign income whether capital is internationally mobile or not. Again, the incorporation of these effects and their repercussions into the model may lead to significant modifications of the conclusions which would follow from the solution of a corresponding single-country model, and introduces an additional element of uncertainty into the domestic decision-makers' universe.

IV. NONLINEARITIES, FLEXIBLE TARGETS, AND THE RATIONALE OF THE MEADE-TINBERGEN-MUNDELL APPROACH

A number of difficulties and limitations inherent in the Meade-Tinbergen-Mundell formulation of the problem of internal-external balance have been discussed throughout this survey; a few of the most important ones are briefly recapitulated here. Tinbergen's Rule, that a unique solution exists if and only if the number of targets equals the number of instruments, applies only when structural relationships in the economy are linear and all the instruments independently and infinitely variable, assumptions which may often do grave violence to the policy-maker's environment. Furthermore, as Niehans [26, p. 897] points out, "these numbers [of targets and instruments] have no economic meaning and can be made arbitrarily large or small just by changing the system of classification."

The fixed-target approach, which is the basis of Tinbergen's Rule and which underlies virtually all the literature on the problem of internal-external balance, is itself subject to serious criticism. Such "representation of social preference by fixed predetermined values of the target variables rather than by a function of such variables" neglects the welfare implications of the policy variables themselves, which may take the form of administrative, allocative, or distributional costs (or benefits), and leaves no room for the possibility that "the object of policy is to achieve the best compromise among objectives and not to maximize the number of objectives that are fully obtained." (Fleming [6, pp. 392-393].)

An attempt to free the consideration of the problem of internal-external balance from the constraints of fixed targets and a linear model has recently been made by Niehans [26]. He points out that the concepts of equilibrium appearing in the literature on this subject, focussed as they are on considerations of dynamic stability, do not in any way imply that an economy has achieved an efficient combination of policies in the (static) Paretian sense, that is, a combination which achieves the highest level of output consistent with a given level of exchange reserves, or vice versa.

To remedy this deficiency, Niehans suggests that the Tinbergen-Mundell fixed-target approach and the Principle of Effective Market Classification growing out of it be generalized in two directions.

First, he suggests that predetermined target values be replaced by a more general social-welfare function that permits a ranking of the relevant bundles of target values and allows trade-offs between them. Niehans himself does not really spell out such a generalized function, however. Rather, his "first approximation" simply makes explicit what is implicit in much of the literature on fixed targets: that, once targets are properly defined, policy-makers always prefer "more" (in this case higher levels of output and exchange reserves) to "less."[54] However, it is not enough simply to regard the targets as variable and then find those policy combinations which maximize one target for a given level of the other. For, as we have seen earlier, linear models yield no such maxima; in the absence of boundary conditions, proper combinations of policies would enable policy-makers to achieve any level of output whatsoever with a given level of reserves or balance-of-payments position. Niehans likens these results to the complete specialization implied by the theory of international trade under constant marginal rates of substitution. Determinacy is achieved only by the introduction of boundary conditions.

This indeterminacy is eliminated by the second of Niehans' generalizations: the introduction of nonlinearities in the effects of policy instruments on targets. This means that the b_{ij} coefficients in Tinbergen's $n \times n$ system on page 3 are no longer constant but variable. Equations (1c) and (1d) of footnote 10 then tell us that the EE and II loci will no longer be straight lines, since the partial derivatives which determine the slopes will vary. Under certain reasonable assumptions about the signs of the second derivatives of these functions,[55] the result will be a curved "target-possibilities frontier" analogous to the production-possibilities frontier of international trade theory. Each point on such a curve represents an "efficient" combination of policies in the sense that it specifies the maximum level of one target that can be achieved for given levels of the other target, just as the transformation curve represents the maximum amounts of one commodity that can be produced for given amounts of the other commodity. By analogy, again, with international trade theory, the following condition

[54] Fleming [6, p. 399] argues that target variables with finite optima are, in fact, proxies for ultimate target variables with infinite optima which do not appear in the system.

[55] Specifically, Niehans assumes that the effects of interest-rate changes on capital inflows and on the demand for cash balances weaken as the level of interest rates rises, that is, that $L_{ii} > 0$ and $K_{ii} < 0$.

for a maximum must hold at every point on the target frontier:

$$\frac{\delta y_1/\delta x_1}{\delta y_1/\delta x_2} = \frac{\delta y_2/\delta x_1}{\delta y_2/\delta x_2}.$$

At this point, of course, neither instrument has a comparative advantage with respect to either target. In contrast to the prescription of the Principle of Effective Market Classification based on the assumption of fixed comparative-advantage ratios, Niehans' generalized version of the Principle prescribes that one should "increase the use of instruments with a comparative advantage at the expense of those with a disadvantage, if possible up to the point where all comparative advantages have disappeared" [26, p. 899]. The selection of the desired point on the target frontier requires more detailed knowledge of the social-welfare function, of the relative priorities assigned to the two targets. But policy combinations leading to points inside the frontier will always be inferior to combinations leading to points on the frontier, whatever the shape of the welfare function.

Niehans' paper represents the only attempt, as far as I know, to remove the problem of internal-external balance from the confines of the linear, fixed-targets approach. This general adherence to the Tinbergen-Mundell model does not stem from unawareness of its limitations on the part of economists concerned with international economic interdependence, including the originators of the model themselves. Nor does it arise from any lack of alternative models to follow. Nonlinear structural relationships have become a feature of many large macroeconomic models. And a great deal of work, associated primarily with Theil [e.g., 38], has been done on the development of flexible-target social-welfare functions, of which the most widely used variant is the least-squares quadratic preference function which minimizes the weighted sum of squares of the deviations between desired and corresponding actual values of all variables with welfare implications. Such a function avoids many of the difficulties discussed at the beginning of this section: it provides a unique solution irrespective of whether the number of instruments equals the number of targets or not, it makes it possible always to find an optimal decision which does not disregard any of the targets, and it provides a simple mechanism for dealing with the problems of decision-making under uncertainty.[56]

[56] When uncertainty can be represented by stochastic (random) components, the "certainty equivalence theorem" guarantees that the *expectation* of the least-

The least-squares quadratic welfare function suffers from conceptual difficulties of its own, of course. One is its symmetry assumption: that policy-makers will always regard positive and negative deviations of the same magnitude from desired values as equally undesirable. In addition, as Fleming [6, pp. 397-401] points out, it shares at least two major weaknesses with the fixed-targets approach: the assignment of predetermined optimal values to variables, such as real income, whose optima are actually infinite; and the neglect of value interrelationships among the variables included in the welfare function.

The real brief for the fixed-targets, linear-constraints approach to the problem of achieving internal and external balance cannot be found, however, in a detailed comparison of its formal characteristics with those of the most readily available alternatives. It lies rather in the particular applicability of this approach to a decision-making context in which authority for economic policy-making is extremely decentralized, governmental policies for macroeconomic stabilization are pursued in a market-oriented rather than a planning-oriented framework, information about structural relationships in the economic system is severely limited, and the likelihood that decision-making rules will be adopted by policy-makers increases in direct proportion to their simplicity. Developed in a politico-economic framework which displays all these characteristics, the targets-instruments approach has led to the recognition of internal and external balance as explicit policy goals rather than as equilibrium states automatically achieved, has emphasized the need to develop new policy instruments or at least free the shackles on existing ones (flexible exchange rates, for instance) if these multiple goals are to be simultaneously achieved, and has encouraged the utilization of econometric estimation techniques as an important adjunct to the formulation of economic policy. Despite the major conceptual deficiencies of the targets-instruments approach, these developments suggest that the very considerable effort which economists have devoted to investigating and extending its applicability to the problems of internal and external balance has been well warranted.

---

squares quadratic welfare function will be maximized when all random coefficients in the system are replaced by their expected values, that is, when the existence of uncertainty is disregarded. See Theil [38].

References

1. Baggott, Nancy and Flanders, M. June, "Economic Policy in an Open Economy: A Reader's Guide," *Economia Internazionale*, Vol. XXII (November 1969), pp. 1-15.
2. Brainard, William, "Uncertainty and the Effectiveness of Policy," *American Economic Review*, Vol. LVII (May 1967), pp. 411-425.
3. Cooper, Richard N., "Macro-Economic Policy Adjustment in Interdependent Economies," *Quarterly Journal of Economics*, Vol. LXXXIII (February 1969), pp. 1-24.
4. ———, "On the Theory of Policy in an Integrated Economy" (1965, unpublished).
5. Fleming, J. Marcus, "Domestic Financial Policies Under Fixed and Under Floating Exchange Rates," IMF *Staff Papers*, Vol. IX (November 1962), pp. 369-380.
6. ———, "Targets and Instruments," IMF *Staff Papers*, Vol. XV (November 1968), pp. 387-402.
7. Floyd, J. E., "Monetary and Fiscal Policy in a World of Capital Mobility," *Review of Economic Studies*, Vol. XXXVI (October 1969), pp. 503-517.
8. Fox, Karl A., Sengupta, J. K., and Thorbecke, Eric, *The Theory of Quantitative Economic Policy* (Amsterdam: 1966).
9. Helliwell, J. F., "Monetary and Fiscal Policies for an Open Economy," *Oxford Economic Papers*, Vol. XXI-1 (March 1969), pp. 35-55.
10. Hickman, Burt G., "Introduction" to Hickman (ed.), *Quantitative Planning of Economic Policy* (Washington, D.C.: 1965).
11. Johnson, Harry G., "Some Aspects of the Theory of Economic Policy in a World of Capital Mobility," in Tullio Bagiotti (ed.), *Essays in Honor of Marco Fanno* (Padua: 1966).
12. ———, "Theoretical Problems of the International Monetary System," *Pakistan Development Review*, Vol. VII-1 (Spring 1967), pp. 1-28.
13. Jones, Ronald W., "Monetary and Fiscal Policy for an Economy with Fixed Exchange Rates," *Journal of Political Economy*, Vol. LXXVI (Part II, July-August 1968), pp. 921-943.
14. Kemp, M. C., "Monetary and Fiscal Policy under Alternative

Assumptions about International Capital Mobility," *Economic Record*, Vol. 42 (December 1966), pp. 598-605.

15. Komiya, Ryutaro, "Economic Growth and the Balance of Payments: A Monetary Approach," *Journal of Political Economy*, Vol. LXXVII (January 1969), pp. 35-48.

16. Krueger, Anne O., "The Impact of Alternative Government Policies Under Varying Exchange Systems," *Quarterly Journal of Economics*, Vol. LXXIX (May 1965), pp. 195-208.

17. Levin, Jay H., "International Capital Mobility and the Assignment Problem," (1969, unpublished).

18. Machlup, Fritz, "Equilibrium and Disequilibrium: Misplaced Concreteness and Disguised Politics," in Machlup, *International Payments, Debts, and Gold* (New York: 1964).

19. McKinnon, Ronald I., "Portfolio Balance and International Payments Adjustment," in Robert Mundell and Alexander Swoboda (eds.), *Monetary Problems of the International Economy* (Chicago: 1969).

20. ———— and Oates, Wallace R., "The Implications of International Economic Integration for Monetary, Fiscal, and Exchange Rate Policy," *Princeton Studies in International Finance No. 16*, 1966.

21. Meade, J. E., *The Theory of International Economic Policy*. Vol. One: *The Balance of Payments* (London: 1951).

22. Mundell, Robert A., "The Appropriate Use of Monetary and Fiscal Policy for Internal and External Stability," IMF *Staff Papers*, Vol. IX (March 1962), pp. 70-79.

23. ————, "Capital Mobility and Stabilization Policy Under Fixed and Flexible Exchange Rates," *Canadian Journal of Economics and Political Science*, Vol. XXIX (November 1963), pp. 475-485.

24. ————, "The International Disequilibrium System" *Kyklos*, Vol. XIV (1961), pp. 153-170.

25. ————, *International Economics* (New York and London: 1968).

26. Niehans, Jurg, "Monetary and Fiscal Policies in Open Economics Under Fixed Exchange Rates: An Optimizing Approach," *Journal of Political Economy*, Vol. LXXVI (Part II, July-August 1968), pp. 893-920.

27. Oates, Wallace E., "Budget Balance and Equilibrium Income: A Comment on the Efficacy of Fiscal and Monetary Policy in An Open Economy," *Journal of Finance*, Vol. XXI (September 1966), pp. 489-498.

28. Ott, David J. and Ott, Attiat, F., "Monetary and Fiscal Policy: Goals and the Choice of Instruments," *Quarterly Journal of Economics*, Vol. LXXXII (May 1968), pp. 313-325.

29. Patrick, John, "The Optimum Policy Mix: Convergence and Consistency," in Peter B. Kenen and Roger Lawrence (eds.), *The Open Economy* (New York: 1968).

30. Prachowny, Martin F. J., "Monetary-Fiscal Policy Mix for the Balance of Payments: The Case of the United States," paper presented at the meetings of the Canadian Economic Association at Calgary, Alberta, June 5-8, 1968.

31. Quirk, James P. and Zarley, Arvid M., "Policies to Attain External and Internal Balance: A Reappraisal," in Quirk and Zarley (eds.), *Papers in Quantitative Economics* (Lawrence, Kansas: 1968), pp. 433-462.

32. Rhomberg, R. R., "A Model of the Canadian Economy Under Fixed and Fluctuating Exchange Rates," *Journal of Political Economy*, Vol. LXXII (February 1964), pp. 1-31.

33. Roper, Don E., "Macroeconomic Policies and the Distribution of the World Money Supply," *Quarterly Journal of Economics* (forthcoming).

34. Saving, Thomas R., "Monetary-Policy Targets and Indicators," *Journal of Political Economy*, Vol. LXXV (Supplement: August 1967), Part II, pp. 446-456.

35. Sohmen, Egon, "Fiscal and Monetary Policies Under Alternative Exchange-Rate Systems," *Quarterly Journal of Economics*, Vol. LXXXI (August 1967), pp. 515-523.

36. Sohmen, Egon and Schneeweiss, Hans, "Fiscal and Monetary Policies under Alternative Exchange Rate Systems: A Correction," *Quarterly Journal of Economics*, Vol. LXXXIII (May 1969), pp. 336-340.

37. Takayama, Akira, "The Effects of Fiscal and Monetary Policies Under Flexible and Fixed Exchange Rates," *Canadian Journal of Economics*, Vol. II-2 (May 1969), pp. 190-209.

38. Theil, Henri, "Linear Decision Rules for Macrodynamic Policy," in Hickman [10], pp. 18-42.

39. Tinbergen, Jan, *On the Theory of Economic Policy* (Amsterdam: 1952).

PUBLICATIONS OF THE

INTERNATIONAL FINANCE SECTION

The International Finance Section publishes at irregular intervals papers in four series: ESSAYS IN INTERNATIONAL FINANCE, PRINCETON STUDIES IN INTERNATIONAL FINANCE, SPECIAL PAPERS IN INTERNATIONAL ECONOMICS, AND REPRINTS IN INTERNATIONAL FINANCE. All four of these should be ordered directly from the Section (P.O. Box 644, Princeton, New Jersey 08540).

A mailing list is maintained for free distribution of ESSAYS and REPRINTS as they are issued and of announcements of new issues in the series of STUDIES and SPECIAL PAPERS. Requests for inclusion in this list will be honored, except that students will not be placed on the permanent mailing list, because waste results from frequent changes of address.

For the STUDIES and SPECIAL PAPERS there will be a charge of $1.00 a copy, payable in advance. This charge will be waived on copies distributed to college and university libraries here and abroad. In addition the charge is sometimes waived on single copies requested by persons residing abroad who find it difficult to make remittance.

For noneducational institutions there is a simplified procedure whereby all issues of all four series will be sent to them automatically in return for an annual contribution of $25 to the publication program of the International Finance Section. Any company finding it irksome to order individual SPECIAL PAPERS and STUDIES is welcome to take advantage of this plan.

Orders for single copies of the ESSAYS and REPRINTS will be filled against a handling charge of $1.00, payable in advance. The charge for more than one copy of these two series will be $0.50 a copy. These charges may be waived to foreign institutions of education and research. Charges may also be waived on single copies requested by persons residing abroad who find it difficult to make remittance.

For the convenience of our British customers, arrangements have been made for retail distribution of the STUDIES and SPECIAL PAPERS through the Economists' Bookshop, Portugal Street, London, W.C. 2, and Blackwells, Broad Street, Oxford. These booksellers will usually have our publications in stock.

The following is a complete list of the publications of the International Finance Section. The issues of the four series that are still available from the Section are marked by asterisks. Those marked by daggers are out of stock at the International Finance Section but may be obtained in xerographic reproductions (that is, looking like the originals) from University Microfilm, Inc., 300 N. Zeeb Road, Ann Arbor, Michigan 48106. (Most of the issues are priced at $3.00.)

†No. 1. Friedrich A. Lutz, *International Monetary Mechanisms: The Keynes and White Proposals.* (July 1943)

† 2. Frank D. Graham, *Fundamentals of International Monetary Policy.* (Autumn 1943)

† 3. Richard A. Lester, *International Aspects of Wartime Monetary Experience.* (Aug. 1944)

† 4. Ragnar Nurkse, *Conditions of International Monetary Equilibrium.* (Spring 1945)

† 5. Howard S. Ellis, *Bilateralism and the Future of International Trade.* (Summer 1945)

† 6. Arthur I. Bloomfield, *The British Balance-of-Payments Problem.* (Autumn 1945)

† 7. Frank A. Southard, Jr., *Some European Currency and Exchange Experiences: 1943-1946.* (Summer 1946)

† 8. Miroslav A. Kriz, *Postwar International Lending.* (Spring 1947)

† 9. Friedrich A. Lutz, *The Marshall Plan and European Economic Policy.* (Spring 1948)

† 10. Frank D. Graham, *The Cause and Cure of "Dollar Shortage."* (Jan. 1949)

† 11. Horst Mendershausen, *Dollar Shortage and Oil Surplus in 1949-1950.* (Nov. 1950)

† 12. Sir Arthur Salter, *Foreign Investment.* (Feb. 1951)

† 13. Sir Roy Harrod, *The Pound Sterling.* (Feb. 1952)

† 14. S. Herbert Frankel, *Some Conceptual Aspects of International Economic Development of Underdeveloped Territories.* (May 1952)

† 15. Miroslav A. Kriz, *The Price of Gold.* (July 1952)

† 16. William Diebold, Jr., *The End of the I.T.O.* (Oct. 1952)

† 17. Sir Douglas Copland, *Problems of the Sterling Area: With Special Reference to Australia.* (Sept. 1953)

† 18. Raymond F. Mikesell, *The Emerging Pattern of International Payments.* (April 1954)

† 19. D. Gale Johnson, *Agricultural Price Policy and International Trade.* (June 1954)

† 20. Ida Greaves, *"The Colonial Sterling Balances."* (Sept. 1954)

† 21. Raymond Vernon, *America's Foreign Trade Policy and the GATT.* (Oct. 1954)

† 22. Roger Auboin, *The Bank for International Settlements, 1930-1955.* (May 1955)

† 23. Wytze Gorter, *United States Merchant Marine Policies: Some International Implications.* (June 1955)

† 24. Thomas C. Schelling, *International Cost-Sharing Arrangements.* (Sept. 1955)

† 25. James E. Meade, *The Belgium-Luxembourg Economic Union, 1921-1939.* (March 1956)

† 26. Samuel I. Katz, *Two Approaches to the Exchange-Rate Problem: The United Kingdom and Canada.* (Aug. 1956)

† 27. A. R. Conan, *The Changing Pattern of International Investment in Selected Sterling Countries.* (Dec. 1956)

† 28. Fred H. Klopstock, *The International Status of the Dollar.* (May 1957)

† 29. Raymond Vernon, *Trade Policy in Crisis.* (March 1958)

† 30. Sir Roy Harrod, *The Pound Sterling, 1951-1958.* (Aug. 1958)

† 31. Randall Hinshaw, *Toward European Convertibility.* (Nov. 1958)

† 32. Francis H. Schott, *The Evolution of Latin American Exchange-Rate Policies since World War II.* (Jan. 1959)

† 33. Alec Cairncross, *The International Bank for Reconstruction and Development.* (March 1959)

† 34. Miroslav A. Kriz, *Gold in World Monetary Affairs Today.* (June 1959)
† 35. Sir Donald MacDougall, *The Dollar Problem: A Reappraisal.* (Nov. 1960)
† 36. Brian Tew, *The International Monetary Fund: Its Present Role and Future Prospect.* (March 1961)
† 37. Samuel I. Katz, *Sterling Speculation and European Convertibility: 1955-1958.* (Oct. 1961)
† 38. Boris C. Swerling, *Current Issues in International Commodity Policy.* (June 1962)
† 39. Pieter Lieftinck, *Recent Trends in International Monetary Policies.* (Sept. 1962)
† 40. Jerome L. Stein, *The Nature and Efficiency of the Foreign Exchange Market.* (Oct. 1962)
† 41. Friedrich A. Lutz, *The Problem of International Liquidity and the Multiple-Currency Standard.* (March 1963)
† 42. Sir Dennis Robertson, *A Memorandum Submitted to the Canadian Royal Commission on Banking and Finance.* (May 1963)
† 43. Marius W. Holtrop, *Monetary Policy in an Open Economy: Its Objectives, Instruments, Limitations, and Dilemmas.* (Sept. 1963)
† 44. Harry G. Johnson, *Alternative Guiding Principles for the Use of Monetary Policy.* (Nov. 1963)
† 45. Jacob Viner, *Problems of Monetary Control.* (May 1964)
† 46. Charles P. Kindleberger, *Balance-of-Payments Deficits and the International Market for Liquidity.* (May 1965)
† 47. Jacques Rueff and Fred Hirsch, *The Role and the Rule of Gold: An Argument.* (June 1965)
† 48. Sidney Weintraub, *The Foreign-Exchange Gap of the Developing Countries.* (Sept. 1965)
† 49. Tibor Scitovsky, *Requirements of an International Reserve System.* (Nov. 1965)
† 50. John H. Williamson, *The Crawling Peg.* (Dec. 1965)
† 51. Pieter Lieftinck, *External Debt and Debt-Bearing Capacity of Developing Countries.* (March 1966)
† 52. Raymond F. Mikesell, *Public Foreign Capital for Private Enterprise in Developing Countries.* (April 1966)
† 53. Milton Gilbert, *Problems of the International Monetary System.* (April 1966)
† 54. Robert V. Roosa and Fred Hirsch, *Reserves, Reserve Currencies, and Vehicle Currencies: An Argument.* (May 1966)
† 55. Robert Triffin, *The Balance of Payments and the Foreign Investment Position of the United States.* (Sept. 1966)
† 56. John Parke Young, *United States Gold Policy: The Case for Change.* (Oct. 1966)
* 57. Gunther Ruff, *A Dollar-Reserve System as a Transitional Solution.* (Jan. 1967)
* 58. J. Marcus Fleming, *Toward Assessing the Need for International Reserves.* (Feb. 1967)
† 59. N. T. Wang, *New Proposals for the International Finance of Development.* (April 1967)
† 60. Miroslav A. Kriz, *Gold: Barbarous Relic or Useful Instrument?* (June 1967)
* 61. Charles P. Kindleberger, *The Politics of International Money and World Language.* (Aug. 1967)
* 62. Delbert A. Snider, *Optimum Adjustment Processes and Currency Areas.* (Oct. 1967)
† 63. Eugene A. Birnbaum, *Changing the United States Commitment to Gold.* (Nov. 1967)
† 64. Alexander K. Swoboda, *The Euro-Dollar Market: An Interpretation.* (Feb. 1968)

* 65. Fred H. Klopstock, *The Euro-Dollar Market: Some Unresolved Issues.* (March 1968)

* 66. Eugene A. Birnbaum, *Gold and the International Monetary System: An Orderly Reform.* (April 1968)

* 67. J. Marcus Fleming, *Guidelines for Balance-of-Payments Adjustment under the Par-Value System.* (May 1968)

* 68. George N. Halm, *International Financial Intermediation: Deficits Benign and Malignant.* (June 1968)

† 69. Albert O. Hirschman and Richard M. Bird, *Foreign Aid—A Critique and a Proposal.* (July 1968)

† 70. Milton Gilbert, *The Gold-Dollar System: Conditions of Equilibrium and the Price of Gold.* (Nov. 1968)

* 71. Henry G. Aubrey, *Behind the Veil of International Money.* (Jan. 1969)

* 72. Anthony Lanyi, *The Case for Floating Exchange Rates Reconsidered.* (Feb. 1969)

* 73. George N. Halm, *Toward Limited Exchange-Rate Flexibility.* (March 1969)

* 74. Ronald I. McKinnon, *Private and Official International Money: The Case for the Dollar.* (April 1969)

* 75. Jack L. Davies, *Gold: A Forward Strategy.* (May 1969)

* 76. Albert O. Hirschman, *How to Divest in Latin America, and Why.* (Nov. 1969)

* 77. Benjamin J. Cohen, *The Reform of Sterling.* (Dec. 1969)

* 78. Thomas D. Willett, Samuel I. Katz, and William H. Branson, *Exchange-Rate Systems, Interest Rates, and Capital Flows.* (Jan. 1970)

* 79. Helmut W. Mayer, *Some Theoretical Problems Relating to the Euro-Dollar Market.* (Feb. 1970)

* 80. Stephen Marris, *The Bürgenstock Communiqué: A Critical Examination of the Case for Limited Flexibility of Exchange Rates.* (May 1970)

* 81. A. F. Wynne Plumptre, *Exchange-Rate Policy: Experience with Canada's Floating Rate.* (June 1970)

PRINCETON STUDIES IN INTERNATIONAL FINANCE

†No. 1. Friedrich A. and Vera C. Lutz, *Monetary and Foreign Exchange Policy in Italy.* (Jan. 1950)

† 2. Eugene R. Schlesinger, *Multiple Exchange Rates and Economic Development.* (May 1952)

† 3. Arthur I. Bloomfield, *Speculative and Flight Movements of Capital in Postwar International Finance.* (Feb. 1954)

† 4. Merlyn N. Trued and Raymond F. Mikesell, *Postwar Bilateral Payments Agreements.* (April 1955)

† 5. Derek Curtis Bok, *The First Three Years of the Schuman Plan.* (Dec. 1955)

† 6. James E. Meade, *Negotiations for Benelux: An Annotated Chronicle, 1943-1956.* (March 1957)

† 7. H. H. Liesner, *The Import Dependence of Britain and Western Germany: A Comparative Study.* (Dec. 1957)

† 8. Raymond F. Mikesell and Jack N. Behrman, *Financing Free World Trade with the Sino-Soviet Bloc.* (Sept. 1958)

† 9. Marina von Neumann Whitman, *The United States Investment Guaranty Program and Private Foreign Investment.* (Dec. 1959)

† 10. Peter B. Kenen, *Reserve-Asset Preferences of Central Banks and Stability of the Gold-Exchange Standard.* (June 1963)

† 11. Arthur I. Bloomfield, *Short-Term Capital Movements under the Pre-1914 Gold Standard.* (July 1963)

* 12. Robert Triffin, *The Evolution of the International Monetary System: Historical Reappraisal and Future Perspectives.* (June 1964)

* 13. Robert Z. Aliber, *The Management of the Dollar in International Finance.* (June 1964)

* 14. Weir M. Brown, *The External Liquidity of an Advanced Country.* (Oct. 1964)
† 15. E. Ray Canterbery, *Foreign Exchange, Capital Flows, and Monetary Policy.* (June 1965)
* 16. Ronald I. McKinnon and Wallace E. Oates, *The Implications of International Economic Integration for Monetary, Fiscal, and Exchange-Rate Policy.* (March 1966)
* 17. Egon Sohmen, *The Theory of Forward Exchange.* (Aug. 1966)
* 18. Benjamin J. Cohen, *Adjustment Costs and the Distribution of New Reserves.* (Oct. 1966)
* 19. Marina von Neumann Whitman, *International and Interregional Payments Adjustment: A Synthetic View.* (Feb. 1967)
* 20. Fred R. Glahe, *An Empirical Study of the Foreign-Exchange Market: Test of A Theory.* (June 1967)
* 21. Arthur I. Bloomfield, *Patterns of Fluctuation in International Investment Before 1914.* (Dec. 1968)
* 22. Samuel I. Katz, *External Surpluses, Capital Flows, and Credit Policy in the European Economic Community.* (Feb. 1969)
* 23. Hans Aufricht, *The Fund Agreement: Living Law and Emerging Practice.* (June 1969)
* 24. Peter H. Lindert, *Key Currencies and Gold, 1900-1913.* (Aug. 1969)
* 25. Ralph C. Bryant and Patric H. Hendershott, *Financial Capital Flows in the Balance of Payments of the United States: An Exploratory Empirical Study.* (June 1970)
* 26. Klaus Friedrich, *A Quantitative Framework for the Euro-Dollar System.* (Oct. 1970)

SPECIAL PAPERS IN INTERNATIONAL ECONOMICS

*No. 1. Gottfried Haberler, *A Survey of International Trade Theory.* (Sept. 1955; Revised edition, July 1961)
† 2. Oskar Morgenstern, *The Validity of International Gold Movement Statistics.* (Nov. 1955)
* 3. Fritz Machlup, *Plans for Reform of the International Monetary System.* (Aug. 1962; Revised edition, March 1964)
† 4. Egon Sohmen, *International Monetary Problems and the Foreign Exchanges.* (April 1963)
† 5. Walther Lederer, *The Balance on Foreign Transactions: Problems of Definition and Measurement.* (Sept. 1963)
* 6. George N. Halm, *The "Band" Proposal: The Limits of Permissible Exchange Rate Variations.* (Jan. 1965)
* 7. W. M. Corden, *Recent Developments in the Theory of International Trade.* (March 1965)
* 8. Jagdish Bhagwati, *The Theory and Practice of Commercial Policy: Departures from Unified Exchange Rates* (Jan. 1968)
* 9. Marina von Neumann Whitman, *Policies for Internal and External Balance.* (Dec. 1970)

REPRINTS IN INTERNATIONAL FINANCE

†No. 1. Fritz Machlup, *The Cloakroom Rule of International Reserves: Reserve Creation and Resources Transfer.* [Reprinted from *Quarterly Journal of Economics*, Vol. LXXIX (Aug. 1965)]
† 2. Fritz Machlup, *Real Adjustment, Compensatory Corrections, and Foreign Financing of Imbalances in International Payments.* [Reprinted from Robert E. Baldwin *et al., Trade, Growth, and the Balance of Payments* (Chicago: Rand McNally and Amsterdam: North-Holland Publishing Co., 1965)]

†   3. Fritz Machlup, *International Monetary Systems and the Free Market Economy.* [Reprinted from *International Payments Problems: A Symposium* (Washington, D.C.: American Enterprise Institute, 1966)]

*   4. Fritz Machlup, *World Monetary Debate—Bases for Agreement.* [Reprinted from *The Banker*, Vol. 116 (Sept. 1966)]

*   5. Fritz Machlup, *The Need for Monetary Reserves.* [Reprinted from *Banca Nazionale del Lavoro Quarterly Review*, Vol. 77 (Sept. 1966)]

*   6. Benjamin J. Cohen, *Voluntary Foreign Investment Curbs: A Plan that Really Works.* [Reprinted from *Challenge: The Magazine of Economic Affairs* (March/April 1967)]

*   7. Fritz Machlup, *Credit Facilities or Reserve Allotments?* [Reprinted from *Banca Nazionale del Lavoro Quarterly Review*, No. 81 (June 1967)]

*   8. Fritz Machlup, *From Dormant Liabilities to Dormant Assets.* [Reprinted from *The Banker*, Vol. 117 (Sept. 1967)]

*   9. Benjamin J. Cohen, *Reparations in the Postwar Period: A Survey.* [Reprinted from *Banca Nazionale del Lavoro Quarterly Review*, No. 82 (Sept. 1967)]

*   10. Fritz Machlup, *The Price of Gold.* [Reprinted from *The Banker*, Vol. 118 (Sept. 1968)]

*   11. Fritz Machlup, *The Transfer Gap of the United States.* [Reprinted from *Banca Nazionale del Lavoro Quarterly Review*, No. 86 (Sept. 1968)]

*   12. Fritz Machlup, *Speculations on Gold Speculation.* [Reprinted from *American Economic Review, Papers and Proceedings*, Vol. LVI (May 1969)]

*   13. Benjamin J. Cohen, *Sterling and the City.* [Reprinted from *The Banker*, Vol. 120 (Feb. 1970)]

*   14. Fritz Machlup, *On Terms, Concepts, Theories and Strategies in the Discussion of Greater Flexibility of Exchange Rates.* [Reprinted from *Banca Nazionale del Lavoro Quarterly Review*, No. 92 (March 1970)]

*   15. Benjamin J. Cohen, *The Benefits and Costs of Sterling.* [Reprinted from *Euromoney*, Vol. I, Nos. 4 and 11 (Sept. 1969 and April 1970)]

SEPARATE PUBLICATIONS

†   (1) Klaus Knorr and Gardner Patterson (editors), *A Critique of the Randall Commission Report.* (1954)

†   (2) Gardner Patterson and Edgar S. Furniss Jr. (editors), *NATO: A Critical Appraisal.* (1957)

*   (3) Fritz Machlup and Burton G. Malkiel (editors), *International Monetary Arrangements: The Problem of Choice.* Report on the Deliberations of an International Study Group of 32 Economists. (Aug. 1964) [$1.00]

AVAILABLE FROM OTHER SOURCES

William Fellner, Fritz Machlup, Robert Triffin, and Eleven Others, *Maintaining and Restoring Balance in International Payments* (1966). [This volume may be ordered from Princeton University Press, Princeton, New Jersey 08540, at a price of $6.50]

Fritz Machlup, *Remaking the International Monetary System: The Rio Agreement and Beyond* (1968). [This volume may be ordered from the Johns Hopkins Press, Baltimore, Maryland 21218, at $6.95 in cloth cover and $2.45 in paperback.]

C. Fred Bergsten, George N. Halm, Fritz Machlup, Robert V. Roosa, and others, *Approaches to Greater Flexibility of Exchange Rates: The Bürgenstock Papers* (1970). [This volume may be ordered from Princeton University Press, Princeton, New Jersey 08540, at a price of $12.50.]